MAKE IT UP

MAKING IT UP

THE VASSAR CLASS OF '65 ON THE CUSP OF CHANGE

SELBY
McPHEE

atmosphere press

Published by Atmosphere Press

Cover design by Matthew Fielder

atmospherepress.com

For
Katrina and Erika

TABLE OF CONTENTS

BEGINNING IN THE MIDDLE:
The Bank Street Conversations

As I approach my eighties and look back at both the turbulent era – the 1960s – in which I came of age, and the unlikely unfolding of my life – and work! – I still wonder how it all happened. I wanted to be a Vassar girl – my brother's wife was, and she was so glamorous to me. I wanted a college degree and I wanted to marry and have children. That was all pretty much baked into the ambitions of the 1950s girl that I was. What I didn't expect was that I would have work of my own, a professional life that would come to define me as much as the domestic life that I had anticipated. And that my life would in so many ways be defined by the social and cultural influences of the era unfolding even as we were walking across the Vassar campus in the early 1960s.

In the winter of 1987, I discovered that I was not alone in my surprise at the turns my life had taken. At 44 years old, a mother of two daughters and right in the middle of an unexpected career, I participated in a group interview with a dozen or so classmates from the Vassar Class of '65. It was to be one of four gatherings to take place that winter, in Boston, New York, Washington, DC, and San Francisco, with the vague purpose of finding out what was on our minds at that point in our lives. What were our issues, our challenges? The idea was that these conversations might generate some themes for discussion at our upcoming 25th reunion.

These questions were interesting to me, and I was pleased to be a part of this discussion. But what I got from the evening was much more: an understanding that I was not alone among my contemporaries in my feelings of vulnerability, of trying, as a woman, to invent a life with new rules for living, new expectations, and no guideposts for the decisions I had been confronting for the last 20 years. How do I manage working, as we needed the income my work provided, and raising children? Am I giving my children enough attention? Am I giving my work enough attention? I began then to want to document our experience.

That evening, in the Boston gathering, we sat in a circle in the elegant, paneled living room of one of our classmates – a teacher and the wife of an Episcopal priest – in the rectory of an Episcopal church on Copley Square in downtown Boston. The interviewer, an academic researcher from Bank Street College of Education, prompted us with questions to provoke discussion, aided by a sound technician holding a microphone on a long boom, which he swung around to record each woman moved to speak.

I've observed that in the right environment, in the right circumstances, women can be relied upon to speak their truths to each other. Our generation had gotten some practice in "consciousness raising" women's groups that were generated by the women's movement in the 1970s. Undeterred by the formal setting and the boomed microphone, we *were* moved to speak about our surprising, made-up lives, invented on the fly by women raised with the expectation that we would be contented wives and mothers, but then were swept up in the ether of the resurgent women's movement, with its challenge to women to reinvent themselves.

Here's a story from one classmate present during that evening in Boston:

I graduated from college and was married soon after that. I had a job for a little while in Boston, then went into the Peace Corps with my husband for a couple of years, came back and started having children, and now we have five.

I found that the very hardest years of my life were the years in my late twenties – when I had young children at home ... I had chosen to have children. I was being supported by my husband. I did not need to work and I would occasionally just challenge myself to go through the day and do everything just as well as I could ... take care of my babies, be the very best possible mother, cook the best meal, keep the house the cleanest, and I would always find at the end of those days when I'd really made an effort to do it right, I would go to bed feeling completely restless, dissatisfied, completely frustrated, and thinking that something was drastically the matter with me, that I had everything that supposedly a young woman could want and it wasn't nearly enough. Something very substantial was missing and I found it hard to explain that to my husband. He couldn't understand why having this wonderful family wasn't everything to me.

What turned my life around was getting involved in something outside the family. It wasn't work for pay. But I got involved in my community and local government, work unrelated to my children, and yet very satisfying because it was making a difference in the town where I lived. I was working with adults for the first time, having been, you know, just isolated with my kids for several years. I found that, for the first time, I was getting feedback myself by working with other adults in a non-family-related occupation.

So, for 15 years I've been working in my community as a local public official, and at the same time I've had my family at home. For years it bothered me when people would ask, "Do you work?" or "What do you do?" and I felt lost. It was very difficult knowing that the women's movement was in full swing and that most of the people I knew, women with young children, were out there, getting paid for their work. And I wasn't. It made me feel inadequate for quite a few years and I'd say that in the last several years, all of a sudden, that just doesn't bother me anymore.

As it did with this speaker, the gathering that evening helped us to give voice to our own yearning for integrity in all parts of our lives: to find independence and agency, to use our own voices, to achieve leadership and mastery in some work that was our own.

Some of us had an idea what work we wanted to do, but the world wasn't ready for us. A classmate from the Washington, DC, conversation told of her own awakening to this fact:

"After college, I wanted to go into the foreign service and study political science. I'd always been interested in international relations. Senior year, one of the few organizations that sent a representative to campus at that time was the State Department. All the international relations majors met in one of those ornate lovely drawing rooms in Main for coffee. This foreign service representative stood up, a man, and started talking about how wonderful it was to travel as support staff in the foreign service and everything. Somebody said, 'We're really interested in the training program for foreign service officers.' And he just sort of went pale. And he said, 'Well, there aren't a lot of women in the foreign service.' Somebody else said, 'How many woman ambassadors are there?' There was one at the time, who did not have a family and was not married. So, times are very different and they've changed very, very quickly. After that I went to the Vassar vocational bureau

and if you weren't getting married and going to graduate school, and I didn't feel as though I wanted to go to graduate school, their suggestion was to go to Radcliffe for the summer and learn to type because you could type and work your way up. And I could write a book about working your way up."

The conversations that night, and the others in other cities, were about the birth of our self-confidence as women independent of our roles as wives and mothers – even as we had those roles, too. The conversation I participated in that evening in Boston would stay with me for more than 30 years. It was an evening that left me profoundly aware that my own made-up, cobbled-together story was typical of the generation of women who grew up as fifties girls raised for a domestic life, but who came of age in a hurricane of social change.

What emerged from those conversations in four cities was the common understanding that we had been an age cohort that arrived in a country on the cusp of tremendous social upheaval – the word "cusp" came up a lot. "We are all playing out 'cuspidness' in our own personal way," one interview participant said. Another pointed out that we had been "hatched" out of Vassar into an alien world. Our parents had wanted us to be good girls who married well. Our professors at Vassar wanted us to be intellectuals. Our contemporaries wanted us to set the world on fire and with what was left, find our own generational integrity. We were "in the front of the wagon train and we didn't know where we were going."

We Vassar graduates were also aware of our own privilege, as one participant from the New York group put so well.

"I'm struck in all this discussion about what a very, very tip of the iceberg we are, emotionally and socioeconomically. How much do we relate to the vast numbers of women our age, to whom a discussion like this would appear ludicrous ... our

choices, how we were formed ... people who don't have the incredible luxury to examine their lives and who just, for whatever circumstances, have to work very hard just to get from day to day. I wonder how much people from our generation were aware of the rest of the world in any meaningful way. When I went to France on a Fulbright after I graduated, there was all this writing on the wall about the war and I said, 'What war?' It was the Vietnam War and I really didn't know there was a war. And I barely knew where Indo-China was. And I think our generation perhaps ... hopefully ... was one of the last at a school like this that was so insulated from much of the world. Maybe it was just me and the people I knew..."

Near the end of the New York conversation, the interviewer summarized the themes of the Class of '65's conversations with these questions: Where is the Vassar Class of '65? What kind of choices have we made? What has "having it all" meant to us? How have we developed our self-image, our sense of self-confidence? What things are most meaningful to us? Ever since that night in Boston, I have thought of writing a book about our particular generational story. Thanks to a classmate, who used the material for an interesting reunion report, I am now in possession of the transcripts from those conversations.

I want to make sense of our lives in the context of history and the social movements we encountered. I focused on my Vassar class, which seemed just the right container for a group portrait of our era. A number of classmates shared anecdotes with me, and I have reported those anecdotes. I interviewed, at length, eight Vassar classmates – Dorsett Edmunds; Sylvia Drew Ivie; Dede Thompson Bartlett; Moira Burke; Elizabeth Ratigan; Deborah Michaelson Kolb; Hope Oliker Hageman, and Rosalind Anderson Nesticò. I also tell my own story as a writer. These women were generous with their stories and I have been inspired by them and by the women who, with moving candor on those evenings, shed light on the fears and fierce determination of a particular group of fifties girls caught in the headlights of an oncoming train.

CHAPTER 1

Fifties Girls

"I'm interested in the all-stars and in the everywoman of our class in a sense because I think each of us is playing out 'cuspidness' in our own personal way. At the same time, I think you could look at us as a group and the way we represent so many different directions because of this very complicated situation that we found ourselves in."

From the Bank Street conversations

On January 21, 2017, with college friends, graduates of the Class of '65 at Vassar College, I joined an ocean of women, men, and children who participated in the Women's March on Washington, DC. It was an exhilarating, thrilling scene to witness: singing and chanting, young and old women and men carrying signs in a sea of pink hats stretching as far as the eye could see across the Mall in Washington, pushing out to Independence and Constitution Avenues and up the numbered streets until there was no place else to go.

Looking out at the scene, I thought of other demonstrations

in which my peers and I had participated over a lifetime filled with other social imperatives that we had felt moved to support, and it occurred to me: Here we were, a bunch of women in our seventies who, fresh out of college in 1965, more than 50 years earlier, had cut our young adult teeth on the civil rights, women's, anti-war, environmental, and free speech movements. Now, in our eighth decade, we were out for one more trip to the barricades. Where have we been ... and how did we get here?

Five years later, even the Women's March seems like ancient history, but for us, there was a resonance, a through-line from our early years as unexpected participants in social change. And it was a celebration, with a sense of urgency, that we shared, for once, with our children and grandchildren, whose lives have been defined by the changes brought about by those movements. I also write for the next generations, so they can see what change we wrought, and, because change is always called for, to inspire them to continue the work to find balance in their lives.

I write about that bunch of women, graduates of Vassar when it was still a women's college, who started life as a cohort of academically inclined girls shaped by the 1950s for domestic lives as smart wives and mothers – and who were faced, upon graduation in the mid-1960s, with an incoming tide of new possibilities for women, especially in the world of work. Our position on the cusp of the women's movement – neither in nor out – has always fascinated me. For most of us, attitudinal changes more often came in the form of small revolutions against the social norms that prevailed during our childhoods in 1950s America. At first, our world, and our dreams, were largely domestic. If we had greater ambitions, we pushed against the cultural expectation that a woman's place was in the home, or perhaps in the classroom, the library, or nursing units in hospitals. As we found our way, we discovered that our personal decisions had political meaning.

We were making it up as we went along.

Redefinition was in the air in the mid-1960s. As adults we demonstrated on the streets for social policies and against government decisions, defining our own moral center. We turned to a new "natural" orthodoxy of childbirth and child-care, horrifying our mothers by giving birth without anes-thesia and then nursing our babies, rejecting the baby formula our wartime mothers had been bullied into using by the formula industry. A few of us moved to rural Vermont or the forests of Oregon in search of an authentic life. At some point, most of us – 85 percent – were a part of the working world. At first, we assumed this would be "for just a couple of years," and we marched off armed with liberal arts degrees capped off with a summer of secretarial courses, only to find ourselves dissatisfied with the limited roles for women in the workplace. Without guidance, and with the naïve expectation that our opinions – as women – would be as valued in the workplace as they were in our single sex classrooms, we chafed at the resistance of astonished male colleagues and irritated bosses, pushing to demand more recognition and responsibility.

Along the way, we married and had children and then had to try to figure out how to work – if we continued to work – and raise them at the same time, or in serial segments of time, without the social network that became available for the next cohort of women a few years later. As we struggled to create lives that combined work with mothering, we bore the judgment of a society that still disapproved of working mothers. At the same time, our contemporaries who had chosen not to work began to bear the judgment of the new generation for *not* working. No matter what choices we made, somebody disapproved. But the exhilaration came from the fact that we *had* choices. The freedom to define our own lives was thrilling, if costly.

It seems important to note that our cohort at Vassar had, with some exceptions, come from privileged backgrounds. Our fathers had professional work, as did some mothers, though most were at home. We were well educated, were raised to aspire to a college education, and had for the most part come from college educated families. Money also gave us more choices than other women, and a degree from Vassar also helped. The "Seven Sisters" women's colleges conveyed a status similar to the Ivy League colleges for men, and probably helped open doors for us. Vassar, in particular, during the earlier part of the twentieth century, had had a reputation for producing brainy, sophisticated women, feminists and troublemakers. Whether we fifties girls would fit that image ourselves was another matter.

The 463 members of the Vassar Class of '65 arrived on campus much as classes had before and have since, as young women who felt privileged to participate in an elite academic experience. A significant number of us had gone to private school, and of those, most had gone to girls' schools. We were from all over the U.S. and 19 of us were from European and Asian countries. Two of us were African American. We had been selected for admission because we had strong high school academic records, and student profiles that on paper seemed to match the college's expectations for serious students. Some classmates remember an atmosphere of high expectations and strong support, and a few remember a warning at our freshman convocation, that first October, when an administrator suggested, ominously, surely as a challenge, that some of us might have been admitted to the college in error. The eight classmates I interviewed, whose stories I will relate in detail, along with my own, a ninth, in later chapters, confirmed that though we all felt a sense of accomplishment in having been accepted at Vassar, we weren't all very focused on what we would *do* with our education.

Though the first three are outliers in a cohort of classmates who were teachers, nurses, librarians, lab technicians, midlevel administrators, fundraisers, bookkeepers, publicists, professors, and homemakers, they provide a dramatic illustration of the stark contrast between what we initially thought we could be and what some of us became.

Debbie Michaelson Kolb, a college professor, came to Vassar from Rockville Centre, New York. Debbie thought she would go to Vassar, graduate, get married, have children, "and eat chocolate," she jokes. That chocolate-eating girl became, over time, a professor and founder of the Center for Gender in the Workplace at Simmons College School of Management, among many other academic titles.

Elizabeth Ratigan, a computer analyst, came to Vassar from St. Paul, Minnesota. She assumed she would, like her mother, get a Vassar education and "just see what happens." A math student at Vassar, Elizabeth came under the influence of a gifted math professor, Winifred Asprey, who took advantage of the proximity of IBM, in nearby Armonk, New York, to introduce her students to one of the first digital computing courses to be offered in American colleges. Computers captured Elizabeth's imagination and launched her in a brand new career in the digital age. After years at the Institute for Defense Analysis, she would become a computer analyst at the Central Intelligence Agency.

Dede Thompson Bartlett, a corporate executive, came to Poughkeepsie from New York City, determined to do well, but with the understanding that she would work hard and graduate, then, after a couple of years, "marry a guy who went to one of the Ivies and would be a good provider." Though it was not part of her plan, Dede would in 40 years find herself at the top of the corporate pyramid and the senior woman executive at two Fortune 25 companies, Mobil Oil and Philip Morris. Her corporate success would enable Dede to become a benefactor to Vassar and other organizations in ways she would never have anticipated.

Some members of the Class of '65, on the other hand, came to college armed with purpose. You could say that the following three classmates were born at just the right time, each with a mission to improve their world that matched the zeitgeist of the era we were about to enter.

Sylvia Drew Ivie, a civil rights lawyer and health advocate, came to Vassar from the academic environment of Howard University in Washington, DC. Sylvia, one of two African American students in Class of '65, learned early from a famous father, Dr. Charles Drew, and an accomplished mother, Minnie Drew, that though she might become someone's wife and someone's mother, she was also expected to, in her mother's words to all her children, "DO something to help improve the community." Throughout Sylvia's career, as a young lawyer at the NAACP Legal Defense Fund, litigating significant civil rights cases, as executive director of the National Health Law Program (NHelp), a legal services organization helping lawyers in court cases that advance access to health care, she had her mother's admonition in mind. Sylvia's story is one of unique access to influence, through the prominence of her family, coupled with the unique handicap, at least at Vassar, of being Black in a white world.

Dorsett Edmunds, physical therapist and activist, came to Vassar from Baltimore, Maryland. Because of her personality and interests, Dorsett, the younger of identical twin girls, absorbed the ethos of the sixties and, by embracing the values of the era, became a beacon of change, a woman who, in her seventies, is still hard at work in the middle of progressive movements. From the Peace Corps to the classroom, from civil rights marches to feminist groups, with a stopover in a Maoist commune, Dorsett gradually narrowed her focus from healing the world to healing the community and then to more holistic medical practices – physical therapy, zero balancing therapy, and acupuncture – that help individuals to take an active role in healing themselves.

Moira Burke, an ophthalmologist, came to Vassar from Buffalo, New York. She also had a plan from childhood, a sense of purpose, having declared her intention in a 4th grade composition: she wanted to be a doctor. A determined, focused girl who excelled in math and science, she was not dissuaded from her ambitions either by the limited resources of her own family in Buffalo, New York, or by the diminished social expectations of women during her childhood. Once through her training, Moira chose to become an ophthalmologist, a specialty that presented an opportunity to build a more flexible practice.

In a new world for women, these six classmates all found their voices and agency, independence and mastery through professional work. All of them married and most of them raised children, and had to figure out how to balance work and family responsibilities. That is part of the story they tell. But not everyone worked for pay. Some members of the Class of '65 found jobs just after college, but stopped working when they married, or when children came along. Embracing a more traditional role in a time of radical social change took equal courage and creativity. It wasn't easy to choose to put family first, when all around you, friends were putting on professional clothes in the morning and getting on commuter trains to go to an office, finding recognition in the public arena. Recognition for what you do is harder to find outside the workforce. One classmate notes wryly, "You can't drive people through a clean bathroom to be admired."

Hope Oliker Hageman, corporate wife, internationalist and volunteer, came to Vassar from Auburn, New York. Hope, providing a counter-story in this book, is defined not so much by our times as by her sense of adventure and curiosity, her embrace of the opportunities and new experiences that her life has afforded her; and especially by the colors and tastes and customs of world cultures in a peripatetic life as a corporate wife. An English major at Vassar, Hope found work to engage in when opportunities arose that captured her interest – working as a reporter for a local newspaper in Malawi, editing a tourist publication in Bombay. Resettled in the U.S., she has been an active volunteer for the League of Women Voters and environmental projects. She never threaded together a career, *per se*, nor did she feel compelled to define herself through paid work.

Rosalind Anderson Nesticò, wife, mother, and breast-feeding advocate, came to Vassar from Tallahassee, Florida. Her focus on family was less a conscious choice than a nod to circumstances in her adopted home, Florence, Italy, where she met her husband, Aldo Nesticò, on a summer trip after college. Her son Filippo's birth would lead to her most creative work as a pioneering lactation consultant in Italy, an unpaid vocation that grew from her exposure, as a new mother, to the work of La Leche League. In taking up that mission, Ros, as an American, would become a leader in Italy of one of the significant movements of our generation, redefining motherhood for our own era.

I, **Selby**, a writer and nonprofit administrator, write, too, from the perspective of my own life. Coming into college, from Philadelphia, Pennsylvania, I had no plans. I worked because my husband and children and I needed my income to live. I worked until my work in public relations for educational organizations had a direction and a focus and a trajectory, until I had a mastery of the skills I needed, and a knowledge of the subject matter of my field. I worked because I had to work, but also because I discovered an ambition to succeed, to learn more, to be given more responsibility, more creative opportunities, and more authority in my workplace. I worked until I could not imagine what it would be like *not* to spend my days in an office.

My own story is in many ways reflective of the themes of my era – and of this book: a dramatic shift in perspective in life plans; an accidental career, built on ambition we didn't expect to feel; an embrace of an alternative, experimental lifestyle (at least for a while); at every turn, a fight we found ourselves taking on against the culture's resistance to women in the workplace, armed with new awareness of the imbalance of power between men and women; a sometimes overwhelming struggle to balance the demands of family and the demands of work; a sense of political responsibility and, finally, a sense of mastery and confidence and personal power.

Looking beyond Vassar, contemporary men and younger women would make bolder gestures of revolt, occupying buildings, protesting, burning bras and flags, sitting in and opting out. In his book *Class Divide,* Howard Gillette offers a portrait of the Class of 1964 at Yale. Gillette tells the stories of some classmates who expected to go into law and business and medicine and who, influenced by the social turmoil of the times, went not to New York or Chicago or San Francisco to make a great deal of money. Instead, they used their law degrees to represent underserved populations, their medical degrees to provide care to people in poverty.

Miriam Horn paints a similar picture of a generation of women somewhat more radicalized than we were in *Rebels in White Gloves*, a portrait of the Class of 1969 at Wellesley College, Hillary Clinton's class. The fact that those women were college juniors in 1968, when many of the most dramatic protests were taking place in the streets and on college campuses while they were at Wellesley makes their experience substantially different from ours. "Unboxed," a documentary film portrait of the Class of 1969 at Skidmore College reinforces the shift that had already taken place for women who were four years younger than we were. Skidmore students interviewed in the film spoke of "wanting it all," of spreading their wings and anticipating the beginning of "something big" when they got out of college. These 1969 graduates had a sense that they were in control of their own destiny, a concept that we, in the Vassar Class of '65, were only beginning to glimpse. Four years of social upheaval had already had a liberating impact on the women who came after us.

Making it Up uses the midlife material from the Bank Street conversations, the individual stories of some classmates who were willing to share them through interviews with me, or in their own publications, to tell the collective story, including my own, of a small cadre of women who graduated from Vassar in 1965, when it was still a women's college, who came into adulthood with no plans to turn that education into a professional life, who nevertheless made sense of the revolutions with which they were presented and became midwives to the cultural shifts that changed our world.

I choose my own Vassar class because of our unique place just at the beginning of the social revolutions of the 1960s and because of the opportunities made possible by our education in what was then still a women's institution, where the faculty had higher expectations of us than our parents had, or than we initially had of ourselves.

I feel compelled to tell our story now from the perspective of our age and place in the arc of our lives, and because, with the #Me Too movement, the Congressional elections of 2018, the election of the first female vice president of the U.S., and the synchronicity of the centennial of American women's franchise, it feels as if we are at the dawn of another surge of power for women – a third wave.

This is the story of what came to be called the second wave of the women's movement. I think of my daughters, now women in middle age, who are part of a generation that reflects the changing expectations of women that we, their mothers, worked through. Both married and both the mothers of sons, they have spent their adult lives in the workplace, pursuing careers that expand their participation in the world. Both of my daughters assumed they would be full partners with their husbands in raising children and sharing in the financial support of their families. Both married men who model for their sons the ways in which men's roles have also shifted as a result of the second wave of feminism, who share responsibility for the management of the household and child rearing.

As I tell the particular stories of a few members of the Class of '65, I am interested in putting our cohort into the context of history: what were the social and historical circumstances of the post-World War II era in the United States? What happened in the first wave of the women's movement, leading to women's suffrage? What happened to all that energy after passage of the 19th amendment in 1920? What was the social and cultural milieu at Vassar College at the beginning of our time there, in the fall of 1961?

Though other classmates will make cameo appearances through the book, the life narratives of Debbie, Dede, Sylvia, Moira, Ros, Elizabeth, Hope, and Dorsett illustrate the trajectory of our journeys on the cusp of change.

But first, the fifties...

CHAPTER 2

Feminism and the Fifties

"My mother never worked, had no social security number, didn't drive. She was always afraid. Nevertheless, growing up on the Vassar campus, where my father was a professor, working with women professors, I felt that women could do anything. I never doubted it. I doubted myself, not womanhood."
From the Bank Street conversations

This quote, from the Bank Street conversations, illustrates the confusing messages and models we had as women, growing up in the 1950s. To understand the Vassar Class of '65, it's helpful to look at the period of our childhood during that decade.

How did we, little girls born in wartime, mostly in 1943, experience the post-war era? We were war babies, a sliver of births from 1939 to 1944, a generation distinct from the baby boomers, the population-bursting group born after World War II, when soldiers, including our fathers, returned home from the war. One thing that distinguishes us is that many of us did not meet our fathers until we were toddlers. Another, one could argue, is that we spent our first couple of years with mothers who were operating alone, without benefit of partners, managing our lives, independent, with agency they would have to give up when their soldier husbands came home. The mothers we little girls knew were women in charge, whether they wanted to be or not – paying bills, changing tires, and replacing fuses. Though I don't have an answer for this, it's interesting to wonder what long-term influence our fathers' absence and our mothers-in-charge might have had on our lives, those years when all the family authority rested in our mothers' hands – until, when our fathers came home, it didn't.

While we were babies, our mothers were managing life with the privations visited on the home front during wartime, when everyday supplies were limited and mobility (gas) and food supplies were controlled by ration cards. Most women no doubt welcomed the end of war and return of their husbands, but went through a period of adjustment, as the men did, and we, too, as toddlers, with a stranger suddenly living in the house.

Dede Thompson Bartlett saw so little of her father, a research scientist at the Brooklyn Navy Yard during World War II, that when the war was over and he was around the house a lot more she asked her mother who he was.

I first met my father when I was two years old. I was a small girl whose world consisted of my house and my yard, my dogs, my mother, my brother Tommy, and Adelaide, the woman who took care of me while my mother went to work. When I was born, Tommy, a 16-year-old, had to drive my mother to the Chestnut Hill Hospital for my birth, using rationed gas, in a wood paneled station wagon. My father, stationed at a naval base in Hawaii then, on the way to unknown destinations in the Pacific, would not hear the news of my arrival until he received Tommy's telegram a few days later. My mother never got over feeling abandoned when my father volunteered in 1943, at the age of 42, to serve as an engineer in the Navy Seabees (construction battalion) for the duration of the war, leaving her with a teenage son and a baby on the way. She was armed to greet him with a battery of resentments when he returned. He, by contrast, was armed with the respect and admiration of the men with whom he had served, after the soul crushing Depression years.

After we met my father, home from the war, at the train station in the fall of 1945, I, for one, understood I had a job ahead of me. At two years old, I began a campaign to win his favor. In a letter to his own mother written from home in the fall of 1945, my father described my flirtatious attempts to claim him as my own. In the letter, he speaks of "Selby, who by this time is very possessive with me ... greets me every morning with a 'GOOD morning, Poppy,' in her most musical voice."

Dorsett Edmunds' father, Page, a chemical engineer, had, as a wartime Navy officer, been trained for high-risk duty. His job was to dive into submarine torpedo chambers to retrieve unexploded bombs. Dorsett describes her father as a man with a strong faith in his own strength and courage, who had proven himself in extraordinary combat circumstances. It was he who set the tone and made the big decisions in the family. Returning home at the end of the war, Mr. Edmunds took charge of the family, now including his identical twin daughters, Dorsett and Mimi, who by then were two years old. Dorsett's mother was willing to relinquish the reins of family life to her husband, but the girls, twin faces and bodies, were a blur to him. It took quite a while before Mr. Edmunds could distinguish Dorsett from Mimi, and that in itself had the effect of depersonalizing Dorsett's relationship with her father to an extent.

Moira Burke's mother, who had been left chronically ill and fragile from a bout of rheumatic fever in her teens, was no doubt also relieved to have her husband back at home. Moira met her father, who had been drafted into intelligence work for the Army, when she was a year old. Born in Buffalo, New York, to an Irish Catholic family, Moira grew up surrounded by an aunt and a cousin upstairs, more relatives next door. When he came home from the service, her father worked as a science teacher in a local high school, and took on extra work – a night shift in a local steel plant, a bartending job at a local hotel – to earn sufficient income for the family.

Not all our fathers were away during the war. Elizabeth Ratigan's father, Russ, a department store executive; Ros Nesticò's father, George Anderson, a newspaper reporter; and Hope Hageman's and Debbie Kolb's fathers, both physicians, were at home with their families. Sylvia Drew Ivie's father, Dr. Charles Drew, was also at home, but participated in the war in his own important way, earning national renown for his work with blood banks during the war.

The end of the war and the return of the soldiers meant the beginning of a new prosperity in the United States as the engines of industry turned to production of domestic goods and infrastructure to meet the new needs of life in the suburbs – housing, roads, cars, TVs, stereos, power mowers. During the war, women had taken men's places in industry, on assembly lines, on transports and in the office producing the wartime materials that brought the American economy out of the Depression. In wartime, men wrote letters home filled with a deep longing for their wives and families. Now the men drifting home, their units disbanded or their ships decommissioned, wanted their jobs back and their women at home, tending to the children and the household. Our mothers, mostly middle class, college educated women, had not much now to do with their educations. And the post-war economy yielded so many new household conveniences – washers, dryers, electric vacuum cleaners, big refrigerators with freezers – that managing a house was a lot less demanding. In his book, *The Fifties,* David Halberstam describes the era as a time when the American dream was defined as "personal freedom on economic terms." It was a materialistic, acquisitive time when many people, mostly white, moved out of the city to build their own houses on their own lots in a new suburban community. That shift was particularly difficult for women, Halberstam notes: "The move to the suburbs temporarily interrupted the progress women had been making before the war in the workplace; for the new suburbs separated women physically from the workplace, leaving them, at least for a while, isolated in a world of other mothers, children and station wagons."

"Normal" was the value that weighed heavily on our childhoods in the 1950s middle class. After the stock market crash of 1929, the decade of economic depression and the onset of World War, our parents were hungry for a life of stability and predictability they did not know in the Depression. The nation's economy rewarded them with the post-war boom, and in place of turmoil, we settled into what historians describe as a compliant, conformist, socially and politically conservative environment. "Togetherness" was a word freighted with importance. We were clinging to each other and to a common culture as if our lives depended on it. And perhaps our parents, who had known economic privation and the social compromise that came with insufficient money, thought they did.

Despite the economic boom, it was a time that was both optimistic, complacent and fearful all at once, a period filled with psychological stress. Our young lives were still cast in the lingering shadow of the Depression and fear of poverty, as well as continuing war. I remember standing terrified in my parents' bedroom, catching my breath at the front page of the

Philadelphia Inquirer, which featured a large photograph of the first battle of the Korean War, in June 1950. I would have been almost seven years old then, just finished with first grade, but such was the anxiety of the era that I, a little girl born in wartime, needed comfort and reassurance from my parents in that moment that war would not threaten our safety. And the memory lingers.

In my house, we were afraid of Russia, communism, and the atomic bomb, racial unrest in the city, polio (until Jonas Salk's polio vaccine was introduced in 1955), what our neighbors thought of us, and financial insecurity. None of these fears seemed small. We knew children with polio, whose legs were encased in metal braces. We were in an arms race with Russia to stockpile an arsenal of atomic bombs, and to develop even more horrifying weapons than the two we had launched to end the war in Japan – and if the Russians bombed us and we bombed the Russians, enough of those bombs would destroy the planet and end the human race. This not insignificant threat was reinforced when our families were encouraged to consider building and supplying personal bomb shelters, and many people began to store canned food and water in their basements or root cellars. My parents thought the small swimming pool in the back yard might, with the construction of a roof, provide a safe haven for us, so we had the beginning of a plan. Air raid drills were a routine part of our lives. At school, we learned to shelter under our desks or in the basement of the school building. My own childhood terror of air raid sirens has left me, a lifetime later, with the permanent habit of covering my ears whenever I am afraid.

In the 1930s, the labor movement and even the early women's movement were tainted with the suspicion of communism. The Communist Party had a certain cachet, though, among intellectuals and progressives, who were willing to attend Party meetings and demonstrate on behalf of workers.

My parents spoke in awe and admiration of friends from the 1930s, Max and Dorothea, who were communists. They joked that perhaps that early contact with the couple would put them in jeopardy now, in the fifties, when communist activity in the U.S. came under such suspicion. In 1954, I daily came home from school to find my mother intensely focused on the television coverage of the House Un-American Activities Committee's hearings, under the leadership of Senator Joseph McCarthy. By demonizing anyone who had ever had a brush with the movement, McCarthy demonstrated how very dangerous it had become to show any interest in communism. The McCarthy era, as David Halberstam described it in *The Fifties*, "crystalized and politicized the anxieties of a nation living in a dangerous new era." We learned to be afraid both of communists and of people hunting suspected communists.

A most interesting part of the 1950s was what happened to women in that decade, and how women's progress was interrupted just as we were growing up, girls learning to be women in a fearful era. A "good" woman would step back from the workplace so that their men could go back to work. Their job was to support their men.

"My mother was not a fifties mother," Dede Bartlett says. "Her own family circumstances left her with only herself to rely on from the age of 12. She graduated from high school with the highest grades in her class at 15 years old. She had been working for only three months when the Crash came, in 1929." And yet, Mrs. Thompson later found herself a victim of the fifties freeze on women. When Dede was still in kindergarten, her mother seized the opportunity, with her husband's urging, to get a college degree in English, taking classes part-time at New York University. By the time Dede was 13, Mrs. Thompson had earned her degree but discovered, to her disappointment, that she was unable to translate her studies into work – there being little room for women in the workplace at that point. Reluctantly, "she fell back on traditional social pursuits like bridge playing," Dede says. And she applied her attention to her only daughter's education. "My mother wanted to teach me to be self-reliant and independent." Those lessons from her wise mother would serve Dede well.

Dorsett Edmunds' mother, Marianna, the oldest in her family, had not been considered college material, instead staying at home at 17 to help raise her brothers and sisters after her mother died suddenly. When Marianna became a mother herself, she took an occasional college course, but she was mostly busy, like other mothers, running a household, volunteering, managing carpools. Looking back, Dorsett cherishes the memory of an active, cheerful mother, who nevertheless did not present a robust model of confident womanhood. "Whenever I went to my mother for advice or direction," Dorsett remembers, "she would demur, saying 'go ask your father.'"

Moira Burke's mother had not gone to college, perhaps prevented by illness, though Moira confesses that she never understood why. But despite her illness she was a "quintessential homemaker," Moira says, who made clothes, baked bread and, with the help of relatives during sick spells, took care of Moira and her younger sister.

Looking back now, Moira remembers that her parents were burdened with work, money issues, and disappointment, like many of our parents, coming out of the Depression. Surrounded by adults with thwarted ambitions, she was determined to have a better life. She had already decided in elementary school that she would become a doctor – a goal no doubt fortified by the discovery, while Moira was in medical school, that her mother's long illness was iatrogenic, caused by medical error in its treatment.

Elizabeth Ratigan's mother, Helen West, had, after graduating from Vassar, earned a master's degree in English, studying Shakespeare at Harvard. She then had a couple of secretarial jobs – at Pingry School in New Jersey, at an oil association in Washington, DC, but all of it was, in Elizabeth's words, just "marking time" until she married, and she married at 27, late for her era.

Sylvia Drew Ivie was six years old when her father was killed in an automobile accident, leaving Sylvia's mother with the proceeds from a life insurance policy generous enough to allow her to stay home with her children and send all of them to college and graduate school. Charles Drew was the famous parent. He had focused his medical research on blood, after graduating from Amherst College and studying medicine at McGill University in Montreal. With a Canadian colleague, he devised and patented a filter, using potassium, that kept blood plasma from spoiling when banked. It was a significant contribution to both medicine and the American war effort.

But it was Sylvia's mother, Minnie, who set the children on their life courses. "My mother was quite heroic and very self-actuating. She believed that you just have to put yourself in the way of things," Sylvia says, with admiration for her mother resonant in her voice. "She began her college career at Cheney State College, a historically Black college in Pennsylvania, and went on to further study at Columbia and Spelman College, the historically Black women's college in Atlanta, Georgia," Sylvia continues. "Then my mother stayed on at Spelman as an instructor of home economics. She was 29 when she married my father." Minnie stopped working at that juncture to become a wife and mother.

Other classmates' mothers set aside their own careers to meet prevailing expectations of women as caretakers. Hope Oliker Hageman's mother provides an example. Hope's father, John, and her mother, Peggy, had met in Memphis, Tennessee, where he was a medical resident and she was a nurse. Hope describes her mother as a free spirit, who, as a southern woman with an unconventional nature, felt a bit like a fish out of water in proper, conservative Auburn, New York. Peggy was most comfortable with an African American cleaning lady, whom she would ask to stay for lunch on the days that she was there. The youngest of nine children, orphaned before she was 10 years old, Peggy was passed around from sister to sister, who collectively raised her, in Mississippi. "Mom's sisters spoiled her, which may explain her unconventional nature," Hope says. But the Oliker household was not free of the sensibilities of the 1950s. Though Hope's mother loved being a nurse and was anxious to get back to the workplace when her children were in school, Dr. Oliker discouraged that idea. The times were such that, "He feared that having a wife who worked outside the home would damage his reputation in the community," Hope says. Good providers did not have working wives. "My mother fumed sometimes, but she didn't challenge his view."

Debbie Michaelson Kolb's mother, also a nurse, gave up her career to raise Debbie and her sisters in Rockville Center, New York. To channel her energy and make use of her expertise, Mrs. Michaelson was a very active volunteer, eventually running Planned Parenthood in their Long Island County. "Interestingly enough," Debbie says, "it was during the time she was active that Roe v. Wade was decided." Debbie admits it took her a long while to come to see her mother's influence as an active woman, particularly regarding her work with Planned Parenthood. "My mother, in truth, was not that available, and not that involved with me," Debbie says. "She was more focused on my father."

Though they now, in retrospect, see their mothers' grit and durability, Debbie and other classmates have said that they "didn't really know" their mothers. The mothers seemed more attentive to their husbands and their general responsibilities as caretakers, rather than their daughters specifically.

Debbie, Hope, and Elizabeth all indicated that it was their fathers who exerted the greatest influence on their lives.

A couple of mothers were bringing home a paycheck. Ros Nesticò's mother worked full-time for the news bureau of Florida State University through Ros' childhood. Because she lived in a multigenerational family compound, in a house built by her grandfather in 1929, Ros and her three siblings would go home to her grandmother throughout her childhood. Her mother did not call herself a feminist, but still she provided a model for a woman involved in the world outside the home. Living in Italy, Ros used her mother's model to engage in her efforts on behalf of breastfeeding mothers in her host country.

Many of our mothers who did not take on paid work volunteered instead, knitting socks and scarves, working for organizations in support of the war. My mother taught in a friend's nursery school, leaving me with Adelaide until I was old enough to go to the school with her. She also served as a volunteer for the Red Cross – though I don't know exactly what her contribution was – wearing a smart brown wool uniform, and doing work that involved our car, which had a big red cross painted on the side.

Before I was born, financial necessity in the Depression had driven my mother, reluctantly, without training or education beyond high school, into the workplace. There she had found a vocation, teaching kindergarten. She surprised herself – she liked working with children and she was good at it. When I was little, she was away from home for a few hours each day, while I was in someone else's care, and soon enough I went to school with her. Though she had not attended college and would have, without hesitation, chosen marriage over a career, my mother seemed to derive satisfaction from her work, and since it only took up a half day away, she had time to be at home, too, so she continued to teach through my childhood and for the rest of her working life. My parents were perennially financially strapped, especially so during the Depression, and they always needed her income. Still, she enjoyed her work, and appreciated the recognition she received from parents of the children she taught.

What happened to our smart, engaged mothers? It is as if some of these women, raised in the years between the two world wars – perhaps fueled by the women's movement still palpable following the passage of the 19th Amendment in 1920 – had sacrificed real ambition to conform to the cultural standards of the 1950s, in which women were asked to go back and tend the family. Their stories show an energy, an interest in participating in the world outside their kitchens, that some had to learn to stifle. They were metaphorically binding their feet, as Chinese women were required to do in an earlier era to adapt to a cultural concept of beauty.

To get a clearer picture of women's lives before the fifties subdued our mothers, and us and, it should be said, our fathers, we need to look at the struggle for women's rights in the previous decades. My generation didn't invent the women's movement, though I think sometimes we thought we did. We were, instead, a part of its revival. That feminism as a political and cultural movement needed to be revived can be traced to the post-war resistance to anything that resembled a disturbance of the new status quo in the 1950s. A brief look at feminist history helps us better see exactly what was lost to women in the fifties.

The early women's movement (the first "wave") did not start or end with women's right to vote. The first public signs of a women's movement came at a gathering in Seneca Falls, New York, organized by Elizabeth Cady Stanton and Lucretia Mott in 1848 to "discuss the social, civil, and religious condition and rights of woman."

Though women had a number of concerns – property rights in marriage, the right to pray aloud in church, and even birth control (all states banned birth control in the nineteenth century), what emerged as a central issue of those early meetings was women's right to vote – a measure that required an amendment to the U.S. Constitution. That was the issue feminists focused on until, in 1918, the House of Representatives passed the women's suffrage bill. That legislation would, in 1920, become the 19th Amendment to the Constitution.

Birth control was more available, thanks to the work of Margaret Sanger in the early part of the century. With the end of the privations caused by World War I, life in the 1920s was a lot more unbuttoned, compared to the late Victorian era that defined the behavior of our grandmothers before the war.

The suffragists had good reason to feel a sense of accomplishment and, with that taken care of, many women turned away from political activism. Women's status and experience of freedom and entitlement certainly improved in the 1920s and '30s, while our mothers were growing up, but for a number of activists, the work was only beginning. Much to the annoyance of politicians, businessmen, husbands and the culture, women advocating equal rights continued to make their voices heard and still refused to accept the status quo. But now there was a split among the activists. One group, the National Women's Party (NWP), was eager to pass the Equal Rights Amendment – the ERA. This amendment stated simply that "Equality of rights under the law shall not be denied or abridged by the United States or by any State on account of sex." The amendment, which has resurfaced as a political issue over our lives, particularly during the 1970s, was the source of disagreement between the NWP, who were interested in a straight-up declaration of women's rights under the law, and a second group, the National American Women's Suffrage

Association (NAWSA). The latter group preferred to conduct a review of laws affecting women with the idea that some special laws – those protecting women with children, for example – should be left untouched. Corporate resistance notwithstanding (why hire women at all if they need special treatment?), in NAWSA's opinion, women needed some protection. So, while women in general worked more, smoked more, had sex more, wore looser clothes and shorter hair and freed themselves from social constraints in the 1920s and 1930s (think of Carole Lombard, Katherine Hepburn and other feisty, outspoken heroines of 1930s films), those two groups of women were carrying forward the work of women's rights. All of this was in the air during the years that shaped our mothers' understanding of their roles in the new world. How might these ideas have influenced them, mostly girls who had been to college or nursing school, before the curtain came down on their lives in the 1950s?

While the NWP tried in vain to forward the Equal Rights Amendment, the other women activists, now identified as "social justice feminists," worked for other issues in the 1930s: creating educational and economic opportunities for women; making room for women's political participation in the country now that they were enfranchised; protecting women from domestic violence; and encouraging companies to consider family leave and provision of child care, in order to make work possible for women with family responsibilities.

In other words, the issues that were current then were still current when we came back to them in the 1960s and 1970s. After the stock market crash of 1929, social justice feminists became active with the American Labor movement gaining prominence during the Depression. Since the labor movement has been connected in history with the growth of the Communist Party in the U.S., it is easy to see why feminists were regarded with suspicion by conservatives a couple of decades later, but their interests lay in the issues of women in the labor force. Women were poorly paid in comparison to the men they worked with, they could be fired as soon as they married, and they were routinely vilified by their male co-workers, who resented the idea that women were taking jobs when unemployment rates were high during the Depression.

In 1937, "girl strikers" at 40 Woolworth stores in Detroit conducted a seven-day sit-down strike for "fair wages and a voice in decisions at work," notes Dorothy Sue Cobble in *Feminism Unfinished, A Short, Surprising History of American Women's Movements.* "Their long list of grievances included abusive and disrespectful supervisors, unpredictable hours, and expensive uniforms," Cobble reports. The Woolworth strike ended when company executives "promised wage increases of 20 to 25 percent, union recognition, and more worker say over scheduling and job retention." Their strike followed the long traditions of the women who made up the International Ladies Garment Workers Union (ILGWU), one of the largest early unions and the first to have the bulk of its members made up of women. The ILGWU had a history of fighting for better wages and benefits for women. Those battles, which have a familiar ring today, were on *before* World War II.

When the war came along, many women (though not our mothers in the accounts told here) had found themselves in the center of things of necessity, working in the war industry while their husbands and boyfriends went to war, earning a living, participating in the engines of the war economy. Imagine, then, what a shock it must have been when the men came home and three million women were fired so that men could have their jobs back. Judging from our own stories, it would seem that our mothers were privileged to wait out the war, privations and rations notwithstanding, at home. Never-theless, gone were the feisty 1930s heroines and in their place were depictions of happy housewives in magazine ads and the harried but contented moms on television shows like "The Adventures of Ozzie and Harriet" and "Leave it to Beaver." The result of the new post-war "normal" was a collective loss of confidence among American women. For many women, the return of their husbands represented a power shift, indeed a cultural shift in their way of living. With a booming post-war economy, they not only didn't have to work, they were discouraged from it – like Hope's mother, who left nursing when she married, or Dede's mother who found that a college degree didn't open doors to employment for her. Women who were college graduates could instead become unachievably perfect housewives and the "cultural leaven" of the family and community.

During the 1950s, we experienced a sense of material progress, when having a nonworking wife was a sign of a man's success. It was a decade of reverence for Freudian theory, one of whose messages seemed to imply that women were by nature weak and passive, and should stay at the hearth. In her book, *A Strange Stirring,* Stephanie Coontz notes "the 'scientific' findings of Freudian psychiatrists ... that any woman who wanted more meaning in life than she found in the kitchen and nursery suffered from psychological maladjustment." Freud's work generated an industry of psychiatrists dedicated to helping women accept their domestic role.

In *Mothers and More: American Women in the 1950s,* Eugenia Kaledin offers a few more facts that characterized women's place in the 1950s. Women could not receive loans from a bank to buy homes, or credit to meet needs. They could not get insurance, make contracts, or serve on juries. Working women did not accrue social security and received no tax credits for childcare.

Her grim statistics and the "dominant myth of their victimization" notwithstanding, in *Mothers and More,* Kaledin's goal is to illustrate that not all women were victimized in the 1950s. While acknowledging that there were few institutional supports in place for women then, she points to women writers who asserted their individuality in literature, women artists whose abstract paintings were a "reaction to the materialism" of the era. Women used their volunteer power to improve libraries, art museums, and participated in the civil rights movement. Exceptional women like Eleanor Roosevelt, Margaret Mead, and Rachel Carson, unsilenced by the age, used their voices to speak to the important issues of the times. In an era when many tenured women professors lost their jobs because they were suspected communists, Vassar's own President Sarah Gibson Blanding, who refused the call to fire faculty, was considered a "heroic defender of academic freedom."

It was Betty Friedan's *The Feminine Mystique,* published in 1963, the spring of our sophomore year at Vassar, that really shed a light – a klieg light – on the era in which we grew up. It was the book that helped revive the women's movement.

Friedan asked how, exactly, women's fifteen-year retreat into fearful femininity happened. Our mothers were not brainwashed or hypnotized into submitting to this retrogressive era. "There was, just before the feminine mystique took hold in America, a war," Friedan wrote, "which followed a depression and ended with the explosion of an atom bomb. After the loneliness of war and the unspeakableness of the bomb, against the frightening uncertainty, the cold immensity of the changing world, women as well as men sought the comforting reality of home and children."

The world was a fearsome place after World War II, and "We were all vulnerable, homesick, lonely, frightened," Friedan concludes. Scarred by the Depression, our parents still felt its shadow hanging over their lives, carrying the threat of new financial woes once the nightmare of World War II was over.

I think it was an interrupted life in which they were treading water until the world found peace and everything got back to normal. It was what happened to the generation of girls they raised that so horrified Betty Friedan in *The Feminine Mystique.*

How did Friedan come to hold up such a devastating mirror to the plight of women in the 1950s, one that would wake them up from their torpor? *The Feminine Mystique* was originally going to be an article on "The Togetherness Woman," which she would write on assignment for *McCall's Magazine.* At about the same time, Friedan and a friend were asked in the mid-1950s to report on the Smith College class of '42, in anticipation of the class's 15th reunion. For that purpose, she drafted a questionnaire for her classmates. The same material would be used for the "togetherness" article. She asked of her now 37-year-old classmates, among other questions, "What are the chief satisfactions and frustrations of your life today?" The responses stunned Friedan. The women were bored, restless, feeling trapped at home, frustrated with the limited satisfaction they found in their roles as caretakers, while their husbands were out in a much more stimulating world. In *The Fifties,* Halberstam notes "she had tapped into a great reservoir of doubt, frustration, anxiety, and resentment" among her classmates, feelings that she was beginning to recognize in herself. What bothered her even more was the contrast between her own classmates and the placid undergraduate girls she found on the Smith campus at that reunion 15 years after she had graduated. When she asked them about their plans for the future, their answers were that they would marry and have children; nothing else really interested them. Friedan wondered what had happened to these girls, occupying the same campus environment that she had found so intellectually stimulating a generation earlier.

Friedan later noted in her book that the women of the

Class of '42 at Smith were "among the last American women educated before the feminine mystique." Before the Class of '42, Smith women married later (at about 25), had fewer children, pursued advanced degrees in larger percentages (40 percent), and planned to go back to work after the children were educated. After the class of '42, the marriage age dropped dramatically, to about age 21. Women had four or more children, and few got advanced degrees or had plans to return to work after children.

McCall's rejected the piece Friedan wrote from that research. *Ladies Home Journal* accepted it but so changed it in the editing process that it showed the reverse of Friedan's conclusions. Determined to tell the story she uncovered, she pulled the piece and sent it to *Redbook*, whose editors were horrified at the anger Friedan betrayed about the trap in which she found educated women. They also refused to publish the piece. It was not a picture that women's magazines, written for suburban homemakers, wanted to present. Friedan would soon begin to see the article's possibilities as a book. That book became *The Feminine Mystique*.

She came to describe the malaise she found in her generation of educated women as "a strange stirring, a sense of dissatisfaction, a yearning that women suffered in the middle of the twentieth century in the United States." She elaborates. "As she made the beds, shopped for groceries, matched slipcover material ... chauffeured Cub Scouts and Brownies ... she was afraid to ask, even of herself, the silent question – 'Is this all?'"

In the process of defining the feminine mystique, Friedan challenged a number of cultural icons, including Sigmund Freud, Margaret Mead, women's magazines, educators and the consumer culture of the 1950s. Mead, who spent much time in her writing trying to reconcile women's biological function with their cultural function had, according to author

Kaledin, lamented that "women were often educated like men, but then denied the right to dedicate themselves to any task other than homemaking." Freud, who was convinced of women's essential passivity, and their jealousy of male power, now interpreted by the women's movement, was in some ways an easy target. Though she did not blame Freud for "inventing" the feminine mystique, Friedan felt it "derived its power from Freudian thought." He was mystified by women, famously asking, "What do women want?" and impatient and a little disdainful of them.

Friedan took on Margaret Mead for celebrating women's biological function as child bearers, showing women's power, by virtue of their biology, in tribal cultures. She complained that Mead offered the 1950s culture a "world where women, by merely being women and bearing children, will earn the same respect accorded men for their creative achievements – as if possession of uterus and breasts bestows on women a glory that men can never know ..." Interestingly, my generation, members of the Vassar Class of '65, came to embrace Mead's celebration of women's biological function, choosing to have our children using natural childbirth techniques, breastfeeding our babies, not as a definition of our gender roles, but as a part of the arsenal of roles, part of the power we felt as women and casting our husbands in support roles in these experiences.

Noting a need for self-esteem and the "desire for strength, for achievement, for adequacy, for mastery and competence, for confidence in the face of the world and for independence and freedom," Friedan urged college women to "make a plan" for their lives. "Only economic independence can free a woman to marry for love," she noted, "not for status or financial support." Noting that the idea that you have to choose between marriage and a career is a myth of the feminine mystique, she assured readers that they could do both, and even at the same time. The only way for a woman to know herself, she said, "is by creative work of her own." Friedan, of course, was speaking of women who had the resources to get an education in order to undertake that creative work.

Her verdict on the decade of the 1950s was hopeful: "In light of women's long battle for emancipation, the recent sexual counterrevolution in America has been perhaps a final crisis, a strange breath-holding interval before the larva breaks out of the shell into maturity – a moratorium during which many millions of women put themselves on ice and stopped growing." *The Feminine Mystique* did not really wake us up at the time. We were college girls immersed in our academic lives. So perhaps, using Friedan's imagery, we members of the Vassar Class of '65 could consider ourselves the larva, except that the shell was cracked *for* us and we crawled out blinking with confusion before we started to grow again. It gives me pleasure to think of the stories my class-mates tell in this book, and of a generation reawakened to the possibilities of women in the latter twentieth century.

And there was another disturbing portrait of the fifties freeze, so resonant with Friedan's findings, that would come unexpectedly from a study, undertaken by the Mellon Foundation, of undergraduates at, as it happens, Vassar.

CHAPTER 3

The Mellon Study

College was a means to an end, an intellectual diversion, and though these girls were talented, they were sufficiently uninterested in their academic pursuits that faculty, disillusioned by the apathy of students in their classes, reported to researchers their great frustration in even trying to reach them.

The Mellon Study

I n her oral history for the Vassar archives, reported in the online publication, the Vassar Encyclopedia, Elizabeth (Betty) Drouilhet, longtime dean of residential life (whose title was Warden) at Vassar, reflected on the 1960s at the college. "Thinking about the sixties, Betty," asked Elizabeth Daniels, then college historian, "what comes to mind?" Her wry answer was, "relief that the fifties are over and done with..."

A portrait of the era Drouilhet had been anxious to put behind her is provided in a troubling study that I first learned about while reading *The Feminine Mystique*. It was a study of Vassar students in the 1950s. On August 31, 1961, about two weeks before the Class of '65 arrived for our freshmen year at Vassar, the Mary Conover Mellon Foundation published the final report of its decade-long research on Vassar undergraduates, titled "Measurement and Evaluation of Change in College Women." In 1949, the philanthropist Paul Mellon gave two million dollars to Vassar to undertake a psycho-social study of what it takes to make a healthy college community. The Mellon Study, conducted over 10 years (and ending just before our freshman year), included extensive longitudinal surveys of Vassar students, faculty and alumnae, asking about, among other things, their personal, academic, and professional ambitions. In what was perhaps a reflection of the Freudian fervor of the era, the researchers hoped to learn the effects of a college education, in terms of personality changes, on the "achievement of a more fully realized free, adult, healthy, clear-sighted attitude toward life." The foundation chose Vassar because Paul Mellon's wife, Mary Conover, had been a Vassar graduate.

The study's conclusions unearthed an unhappy profile of Vassar girls in the 1950s. Its findings were very similar to Friedan's observations of students on the Smith College campus prior to her 15th college reunion there in 1957. The preponderance of the young women interviewed in the Mellon Study at Vassar had as their single ambition to find a husband. College was a means to an end, an intellectual diversion. Though these girls were talented, they were sufficiently uninterested in their academic pursuits that disillusioned faculty told researchers of their frustration in even trying to teach them.

Vassar students were lucky. In that campus environment, there were plenty of women in leadership and in the classroom to provide professional role models they might aspire to follow. In her 1951 article, "The Vassar Girl," in *Holiday* magazine, author Mary McCarthy, a 1933 graduate, wrote of the faculty she had known while there, who inspired "the idea of excellence, the zest for adventure, the fastidiousness of mind and humanistic breadth of feeling" that informed academic life at the college. She was devoted to Vassar's female professors and Vassar's commitment to women teachers. Imagine the frustration of those professors, as expressed by Drouilhet, when they discovered the apathy of the bright young women sitting in their classrooms in that transitional decade.

In a May 1959 article in *The Vassar Chronicle*, a campus publication, Mervin Friedman, a lead researcher for the Mellon Study, joined his co-writer and researcher John Bushnell in noting, "One of the outstanding cultural developments in this country since the turn of the century has centered upon a redefinition of the image and role of a woman." He added, "there existed in the nation's consciousness ... that a new concept of womanhood was in the making." But after 10 years of research with Vassar undergraduates, they conclude that "First, a requiem must be held for the feminist cause. College students of today ... consider the battle for women's rights to be a completely dead issue."

Friedman and Bushnell affirmed that Vassar students "believe in the prerogative of every person, male or female, to aspire to whatever position he or she wishes," but that women continuing to "scale the remaining male strongholds" needed to forgo marriage and children to do so. Data from the study indicated Vassar students' "clear cut preference for a man's world."

"A future characterized by increasing independence for women is viewed with overtones of anxiety and discomfort," Friedman and Bushnell conclude, adding "The concept of the ideal woman is swinging from its former position of independent and equal to dependent and unequal with respect to the male."

From my perspective some 60 years after Friedman and Bushnell reported their research, these conclusions are shocking enough to make me suspicious of the researchers, all male, themselves. Were they so biased about women's place that they heard what they wanted to hear? But the data, the culture of the 1950s, and even the frustration of Vassar faculty seem to confirm what they say. And they saw at Vassar what Friedan saw at Smith. In her book, she quotes a psychology professor who said of Smith undergraduates, "they're bright enough ... but they just won't let themselves get interested. They seem to feel it will get in their way when they marry the young executive and raise all those children in the suburbs."

Mary McCarthy drew similar conclusions in her *Holiday* article, "The Vassar Girl." McCarthy, who had such fond memories of Vassar faculty during her years there, in 1951 used her dreaded pen to described the students as follows: "the average Vassar graduate had two-plus children and was married to a Republican lawyer ... Vassar graduates are unhappy and frustrated because the college did not prepare them for a life of dishwashing and babies ... The vivid and extraordinary student, familiar to the old teachers and the alumnae, is, at least temporarily, absent from the scene." McCarthy's article, in draft, encountered a lot of resistance from the college public relations office, whose representatives tried very hard to get *Holiday* to edit or shelve the piece. They were unsuccessful.

To measure the emotional development of Vassar women during their college years, Mellon Study researchers surveyed and interviewed members of six entering freshman classes, and six graduating senior classes, during the decade of the 1950s, along with several classes of alumnae going all the way back to 1904, and Vassar faculty. Since the surveys were required of students, the researchers had the benefit of virtually 100 percent response to questions about student attitudes toward careers, marriage, women's roles in society, family, politics and religion.

What the study uncovered must have been profoundly discouraging, if not altogether surprising, to Vassar faculty. While they were not anti-academic, Vassar students had little interest in independent achievement or the development of personal identity outside the definition of wife and mother. Psychologist and author Nevitt Sanford, who ultimately led the study at Vassar, reports in his book *The American College,* "Vassar girls, by and large, do not expect to achieve fame, make an enduring contribution to society, pioneer any frontiers, or otherwise create ripples in the placid order of things."

"Since the validation of femininity and a full realization of the potential of womanhood is thought to reside almost exclusively in the realm of marriage and family," Sanford adds, "there is ... a corresponding diminution of interest and involvement in the intellectual, creative, and allied pursuits." Young alumnae reported that a number of them had achieved success in early careers – they found less competition for achievement after college than they did on campus, and employers seemed to recognize the value of a bright, well-educated young woman. But 70 percent had left work to marry within three years of graduation. They were generally content with their domestic lives, had few of the conflicts between work and family that had afflicted first-wave feminists, and were "hard at work helping their husbands in whatever ways they could." Students regarded it as "almost inconceivable" that they would not marry, and they embraced the idea that a man should be more important in the family structure. If sexual freedom may be included in a concept of feminism, as it was in the 1920s, it is useful to add that Vassar students in the 1950s believed in chastity before marriage – an assumption questioned in dramatic form during our freshman year at Vassar. Nevertheless, the Mellon Study reported that about 25 to 30 percent of students admitted to premarital sexual experience, though the researchers hastened to add that most of those students were engaged to be married.

When questioned about their opinions of higher education, students reported their preference for a liberal arts education as opposed to a technical/professional education, as it enabled them to explore wider interests in order to be more active and engaged citizens. Sanford reported that college was perceived as "enabling [a woman] to attain a fuller life in the future family pattern." They would be better informed wives, mothers and community volunteers armed with a Vassar degree.

The feminism of the earlier twentieth century was dead, the researchers reported with evident relief. "While few people would deplore the demise of old-time feminism, in the sense of a woman's having to prove that she was as good as a man," the report notes that there were some advantages to the earlier feminist movement. "To some extent it provided an alternative to marriage, a way of life for a woman who was unsure as to whether she wanted to marry or at least was in no hurry to marry." Nevitt Sanford confirmed Friedman and Bushnell's assessment in their 1959 *Vassar Chronicle* article, describing the attitude toward feminism in the 1950s as not only of no interest to young women; he found them to be anti-feminist. He reports that, though not feminists, "many students, perhaps a third, are interested in graduate schooling and in careers ... few, however, plan to continue with a career if it should conflict with family needs." The girls and young alumnae were clearly reluctant to pursue anything that might delay or get in the way of marriage.

For some contemporary Vassar students in the 1950s, this might have created a counterpoint to the attitudes of their mothers or grandmothers, and certainly the female faculty at Vassar, who were raised in a feminist era in the earlier years of the twentieth century, who lived through the freedoms for women in the 1920s and the demands for even educated women to work in the Depression and during World War II. Before 1942, the study reports, two-thirds of Vassar graduates went on to further study. All of this further substantiates Friedan's research about women at Smith.

The Mellon Study confirmed the worst fears of the Vassar faculty, who found many of the students, while not anti-intellectual, were not that invested in their academic work. College faculty, according to Friedan, reporting on the Mellon Study and her own research for *The Feminine Mystique*, began to wonder why they were bothering to share their passion for their subjects with these young women, recalling the days when college girls were "out to change the world."

Elizabeth Daniels, retired Dean of Studies at Vassar, reports in the online *Vassar Encyclopedia* that there was a continuing debate at 1950s faculty meetings about the aims of the college as they were defined in the college catalogue. One professor suggested that one of the aims should be to "prepare students for graduate school." That idea was vetoed by the chair of the Vassar Board of Trustees, who was in attendance at the meeting. It was not a goal that would reflect the ambitions of the students or their parents. In the aftermath of the war, Daniels said that faculty became aware that students were looking at college as a stepping stone to marriage, and the college, committed to education, affirmed that it existed to support the "joy of learning for the sake of learning."

Though I don't remember any such courses at Vassar, Friedan says that at some women's colleges, faculty met to study how they could adjust their courses to be more useful in preparing women for marriage and family life. She even suggested that some colleges were introducing nutrition courses to assure their graduates would be wiser cooks, for example, or courses in psychology for parenting. In those years, Vassar's child study department was well regarded for preparing students for teaching, however, rather than for parenting. The department would later be absorbed by the psychology department. Friedan reports that Vassar President Sarah Blanding even "predicted the end of all the great American women's colleges which pioneered higher education for women."

It should be noted that the messages, even from academic leaders, must have been confusing. In 1950, Miss Blanding joined two other presidents of women's colleges to caution young women that their "first responsibility is to the children," though one of them, Millicent McIntosh, president of Barnard College and a noted feminist, also said "women make better mothers if they do not spend all their time on the physical care of their children." Friedan, however, reported that "the one lesson a girl could hardly avoid learning, if she went to college between 1945 and 1960, was *not* to get interested, seriously interested, in anything besides getting married."

Finally, Vassar faculty found the invasion of Mellon Study researchers on campus irritating in the extreme, with their endless meetings, their demands on student time, and their unwelcome counseling of faculty. Daniels noted in her *Vassar Encyclopedia* interview that the faculty became deeply weary of the "saturation of psychiatric approaches, psychiatric jargon" and "committee meetings around the clock."

In the end, the study found plenty of evidence of an emotional maturing process that took place among students between freshmen years and senior years. But while seniors were more confident and self-motivated and self-assured than they were as freshmen, they were also more anxious about their future and the choices that lay ahead of them. Researchers wondered if the current retreat into marriage and traditional femininity might indeed be a retreat in order to remove themselves from a more undefined, uncertain future. It was as if they could lose themselves in a large traditional family life, allowing themselves to continue to be defined by external social expectations, rather than defining themselves as independent individuals. Was this a reflection of their upbringing in the risk-averse 1950s, the strange breath-holding interval that Friedan identified as a stage, a counter-stage in the women's movement, before the next leap?

The Mellon Study researchers did, upon reflection, wonder what would induce further growth in these educated women who had retreated into domestic life...how their education might be "put to a nobler purpose." More should be expected of intellectual, educated women, they thought. And there was the increasingly publicized problem of unhappy women in middle age, who, having raised their children, felt bored and trapped in the domestic lives they had created. These women were said to be at risk of becoming alcoholics or subject to any number of mental health issues. The Mellon Study researchers wondered if "something could have been done" during their college years to prevent this difficulty in later life.

Sanford said, "American society is rather a long way from providing a means whereby an educated woman may combine with relatively little conflict or effort the role of wife and mother with that of professional or career woman." This unhappy truth – specifically the lack of institutional or societal support for working mothers – continued to be demonstrated for the women of the Class of '65, as our own adult stories bear out, and even for *our* daughters now. Sanford added that American society was in need of substantial reform. *The American College,* the book in which he reported much of the Mellon Study research, was published in 1962, but Friedan, whose *Feminine Mystique* was published a year later, in 1963, was already way ahead of him. She had read the final report of the Mellon Study published in 1961. She had already discovered that unhappy group of educated women, now in middle age, who jumped at marriage before they had a chance to define themselves after the war and were now languishing in the feminine mystique she had named, belatedly looking for definition. Friedan sought to expose what she found and wake the world up to the unfinished work in the development of women. It was Friedan's book that moved American society along faster than Sanford could have predicted.

We members of the Class of '65, entering Vassar just as the final report of the Mellon Study was released, remained largely oblivious to its work and its effect on the faculty we were about to meet. But something must have been in the air. Mrs. Drouilhet's quote at the beginning of this chapter articulating "relief" that the fifties were over certainly reflects the tedium and conflict generated by the Mellon Study. But more than that, it demonstrates an early hint – and hope – of the change in women's perspectives that was to come. In the *Vassar Encyclopedia*, Drouilhet recalled a story of a day in 1960 that she called "the most dazzling experience I think I had in my time in office."

That day, in March 1960, a group of five or six students arrived at her office with a plan to picket the local Woolworth's in Poughkeepsie as a gesture in support of the famous lunch counter sit-in by Black students at the Woolworth's in Greensboro, North Carolina. That event, which had taken place a month earlier, would be pivotal in the civil rights movement. They had come to Drouilhet to get permission to picket. "I tried to keep a straight face," she reported, laughing, "having been at college during the days when students acting on national problems didn't go and ask permission!" Asking the students for time to consider their request, "I tore out to Sarah Blanding (president) who in her day was also a radical, and I said 'Sarah, it is the surprise of all time. Our students are still so much in that lethargic, formal, placid state that I just had a group request permission to picket Woolworth's!'" Noting that in their younger days, both Mrs. Drouilhet and Miss Blanding had marched for national causes, Drouilhet gave the students permission, along with a "Drouilhet's 105 in picketing:" keep to the letter of the law, keep walking to avoid a citation for loitering, don't get in any fights, don't dress outlandishly, and "good luck to you." Drouilhet and Blanding later jumped in a car and drove down Main Street in Poughkeepsie, parking near the demonstration to surreptitiously watch the students – and breathe a sigh of relief that the 1960s might give them students reawakened to the world around them.

CHAPTER 4

College Years

"I felt that Vassar gave us a sense of identity as women. It embellished, enhanced, and fortified the idea that you as a female are important, and can contribute to the world."

From the Bank Street conversations

R eflecting on the Woolworth demonstration in the spring of 1960, not to mention the reports from the Mellon Study on campus, Elizabeth Drouilhet, the Warden, said, "It was a great, great relief to me, for I thought maybe the students can take some interest in something except their own mental health." Drouilhet noted that the picketing was a tiny tip of the iceberg in what she hoped could be expected from the new generation of young people coming of age in the 1960s. In many ways, the times themselves reinforced Vassar's message to us that we women had an obligation to make a contribution to the world. Implicit in the social movements developing in the 1960s was the idea that we citizens could have an impact, that we could change what was wrong in American society. We had to take action, to work for change to happen. But if that was the message, we were slow to respond. In the fall of 1961, we were still fifties girls.

The Vassar Class of '65 arrived on campus much as classes before and for a couple of years after: young women who felt privileged to participate in an elite academic experience. The classmates I interviewed confirmed that we all felt a sense of accomplishment in having been accepted at Vassar. We weren't all focused on what we would do there. Neither was the college, though I think our professors, many of them women, might have assumed that their example would provide a blueprint for us to reach beyond the barriers the 1950s had imposed on us. Despite these professors' hopes for us, four years later when we began to think about work after graduation, we went to see Mrs. Johnson in the vocational office. She suggested that if we weren't planning to go to graduate school to get teaching or nursing degrees, we should look at the Radcliffe summer secretarial program, a course that provided useful office skills for many Seven Sisters graduates over the years.

Debbie Kolb, the Simmons professor, admits she worked only as hard as she needed to in order to earn a bachelor's degree in history at Vassar. But she readily acknowledges she was more interested "in boys and having fun," going to the Dutch, a popular pub just off campus in Poughkeepsie. New York State was unusual in the 1960s for being one of the few states to allow 18-year-olds to drink alcohol, and though we could not drink on campus, we were free to drink at the Dutch, and many of us did.

We were still schoolgirls growing up. In each dormitory we voted annually to wear bathrobes rather than have male guests in the dining room for breakfast (this vote was always unanimous in my dorm – we didn't want men around in the morning), but we dressed in nice skirts and blouses for dinner.

After dinner we went to the dorm living room for demitasses and bridge games, foursomes sprawled all over the living room floor and furniture night after night after night, before retreating to study. Though we each had dormitory "jobs," scraping dishes, for example, and emptying cafeteria trays, our lives were managed by "white angels," women in white uniforms who would be at the front desk managing access to the dorm. Boys were allowed in our dorm rooms between noon and 6 p.m., and then only with the room's door open. Everyone was required to have "one foot on the floor," which presumably would have made lying down, and all that could happen then, more difficult.

The first week we were on campus freshman year, we bought used bikes from a local bike shop for our transportation across campus, signed the official matriculation book, and registered for fall semester classes, including Fundies, a required freshman physical education course. The shocker was that the course, formally called Fundamentals of Body Movement, took place with a traumatizing prerequisite – posing nude for a posture picture – during our first week of school.

Fundies provided instruction in the theory and practice of body mechanics, posture exercises, and a physical education requirement of two weekly hours of activity – sports, calisthenics, and dance, for example. The class also included a swim test, as the ability to swim was a requirement for a Vassar degree four years hence.

Fundies is worth a story on its own. The class began with an examination of each student's posture, weight, height, and body type (ectomorph, mesomorph, and endomorph, now discredited terms) and, depending on findings, a program of corrective posture measures, including lying on posture boards, doing abdominal exercises, walking with books on our heads, practicing tiptoe marching, doing knee bends, and standing like a statue. Certainly, part of the rationale for Fundies was to reinforce ladylike behavior by learning how to sit with straight backs, get in and out of a car gracefully, and lift a suitcase to the overhead rack on a train without hurting our backs. In the words of one writer for an August 1965 edition of the student newspaper, the *Vassar Miscellany News*, "'Fundies' is the affectionate nickname for Vassar's Vic Tanny course where freshmen learn to preserve that Vassar look of sophistication." Vic Tanny, a pioneer of the modern fitness club, was instrumental in bringing the idea of fitness training out of the sweaty, rough era of gyms for body builders.

The story of Fundies necessarily begins with the traumatizing part, the examination of our posture via nude photos, because it was these photos that would determine our course of instruction. My memory calls up a scene that is something like this: searching a campus map, my roommate Pam and I found our way to Kenyon Hall, Vassar's physical education building then. There, in the dark gymnasium, we reported for our first Fundies class. After being weighed and measured, we removed all our clothes in a locker room, put on what was called an "angel robe" (a thin white robe with a tie that we were given for the purpose) and, standing in line in this dark place, with dust motes dancing in the daylight piercing the gloom through clerestory windows above us, we awaited our turn to pose for a posture picture. Entering the relative "privacy" of the photo booth, a space surrounded by movable barriers, one at a time we took off our robes and stood naked while a stranger behind a camera (whom we later learned was physical education instructor Ruth Timm) photographed our nude eighteen-year-old bodies from the side and back. We were told that if you had your period, you would be allowed to wear underpants. I imagine quite a few of us lied about that.

Soon, we were given to understand that each of us would meet privately with Miss Timm to study our nude photos and discuss posture issues revealed by them, and together we would plan our personalized program of corrective measures. I have to admit that, if it even happened, I have completely blocked memories of this meeting, the idea of which remains too awful to contemplate. This is not to disparage Miss Timm, a fitness instructor at Vassar from 1944 until 1978, who at that time was assigned to work with students who were physically limited in their ability to participate in physical activity. The Fundies class, which focused especially on those of us with poor posture, fell in her area.

The "posture pictures" story would be treated in an entertaining *New York Times Magazine* retrospective piece, "The Great Ivy League Nude Posture Photo Scandal," in January 1995. The use of nude photographs to study posture was not unique to our age cohort or to Vassar itself. One friend remembers being photographed nude as a four-year-old at Yale's nursery school and others remember similar posture photographs taken at their private girls' schools before they went to college. Similar studies were done at Groton School in Massachusetts, then a single sex boarding school for boys, and probably more secondary and even primary schools. Vassar, in fact, had been taking posture photographs, though probably not in the nude, as part of its physical education program since the late nineteenth century.

Still, so many questions come to mind. What was the rationale for the requirement that we give up a portion of our academic life to the study of proper deportment? To help us look like proper young ladies, carrying our status on straight shoulders? What fading value did this represent in the early 1960s? Why the nude photos? And why did we submit, we docile girls and our compatriots at Smith and the men at Yale, along with other schools, to that embarrassment? This is a question we of the Fundies era have been asking ourselves for a very long time.

Whatever Vassar's motivation was in teaching good posture, the college had a tradition, from its beginnings, to attend to students' minds and bodies simultaneously. Matthew Vassar's 1865 vision for a female college included a strong focus on physical activity to bring balance to students' lives. In Vassar's online encyclopedia, Vassar historian, Colton Johnson, notes that, "in the nineteenth century, common speculation maintained that college attendance would lead to female infertility," the theory resting on the idea that "the human body was a closed energy system" and women's energy spent thinking would take away from their energy to reproduce. The same theory apparently did not apply to men and their ability to think and also fulfill their reproductive function.

As it happens, Fundies was on its way out of the curriculum while the Class of '65 was at Vassar. Each year's course catalogue from those years shows fewer hours required of freshmen and sophomores for physical activity, and by 1968, Fundies was no longer listed in the catalogue. When Vassar began to admit men, in 1969, there was no longer any physical education requirement. This in turn reflected the growth of competitive team sports among college women as well as men.

What brought us to Poughkeepsie in the fall of 1961? I was powerfully influenced by my older brother, whose wife had gone to Vassar, and from an early age, I set Vassar as a goal for myself. I was thrilled when I was accepted at this school that I had long viewed in a golden aura, fitting for my sister-in-law. Once there, even without one ounce of professional ambition, I, too, recall being hungry for the college's academic offerings. Joining the melee at the registrar's office that first week to register for freshman courses, I began to taste the profound freedom the college offered: to try anything, beyond core requirements, that sounded interesting to me. Our limited vision notwithstanding, the college years were going to be an academic feast. I think one thing Vassar had banked on was our intellectual curiosity.

For Dede Thompson, the corporate executive, Vassar was an easy choice. Women's colleges were understood to provide the best education for girls at the time, and Dede was coming out of a girls' school, so "it seemed very natural." From college, Dede wanted what many of us hoped for – intellectual development, wisdom, social and cultural sophistication, a husband and, vaguely, some career training. Her parents expected Dede to graduate from college and assumed she would marry after school. Dede reports that when her father learned, in her sophomore year, that some students suffered from an "identity crisis," he made it clear that "I could have any identity crisis I wished, as long as it wasn't on his time and his dime." Dede buckled down. Because it was her dream to spend her junior year in Paris, she majored in French, instead of the major that interested her most, history.

Hope Hageman, the world traveling corporate wife, had applied to and was accepted at Cornell, but under pressure from her father, she settled on Vassar, another New York school where she could use the state Regents Scholarship she had been awarded. She was surprised and gratified, she says, to discover at Vassar "so many women who were like me," who showed some independence in their thinking. Though she remembers she was so taken with college that her grades slipped for a while, Hope found Vassar to be a "joyous experience," with so many courses to choose from, and so much intellectual stimulation. "What I loved," she says, "was not so much that we were learning what answers to give, but rather what questions to ask. We were learning to dig deeper, with each set of information to ask for more." Hope remembers that her political science professor, Wilfred Rumble, was especially effective in challenging students to expand the scope of their understanding. Hope's hunger to reach for more would define her life of adventure after college.

Sylvia Drew Ivie, the civil rights lawyer, had an entirely different experience. Her introduction to the Vassar community – and perhaps an unheeded tipoff – came when three alumnae visited Sylvia's family at their house in Washington, DC. Sylvia describes the scene. "Three ladies came to see us in our home, and I immediately had the impression that they had never been in a Black household before. When I saw them sitting stiffly, knees together, clutching their purses, I was put off by their fearful behavior," Sylvia remembers. "To my mother's annoyance, I slouched in my chair and didn't try very hard. There was nothing in my house for those women to be afraid of!"

Sylvia, nevertheless, liked being in a women's college. She liked the feeling she had of the power of women at the school. Many of the professors were women, and the girls spoke up in class. She recalls the informality of one history professor, Rhoda Rapparport, who, abandoning the formality of classroom behavior, came and sat on the front of her desk, legs swinging slightly, and addressed the class from a more intimate distance that felt to Sylvia like "an electric moment," an injection of warmth between faculty and students. That all felt good.

But "I basically staged a four-year sit-in," Sylvia admits. Why? Her resentment about the college grew from the fact that, despite indicating her desire for a roommate in a summer questionnaire, she was surprised to find, when she got to school, that she was given a single room. After a little research with the few Black students on campus, Sylvia soon learned that Vassar had, since the 1940s, been admitting one or two Black students in each class, and that all the Black girls were housed in singles. Wanting to address this policy, Sylvia reached out, unsuccessfully, to the other Black student in the Class of '65, Peggy Dye. Peggy, who had also been given a single room, sequestered herself from social interaction, including with Sylvia. "Peggy had a prominent 'do not disturb' sign on her door, and it stayed there while she was at Vassar," Sylvia remembers.

She decided to go to the dean, Mrs. Drouilhet, to address her discontent about her room. She went to the Warden's office and asked her secretary for an appointment. "She asked me, 'What would you like to see the Warden about?'" Sylvia remembers. "I said I'd prefer to discuss my issue privately with Mrs. Drouilhet, and the secretary turned down my request. Twice more I went in and asked for an appointment, and the third time, when the secretary asked me why, I said, 'To discuss racial discrimination.' I got the appointment right away."

Sylvia goes on to describe the meeting with Mrs. Drouilhet, whose self-possession and sophistication made her almost as intimidating as her title. "I remember sitting across from the Warden's desk and looking at a tall, erect woman who had hairs coming from her chin, who smelled of cigarettes, and who looked at me coolly when I asked her why the college had asked me about my preferences for a roommate when they already knew that they would not put me in a shared room."

"You have to understand, Sylvia," she quotes the Warden saying, "that we need to consider the sensitivities of the southern girls when assigning roommates."

"What about my feelings?" Sylvia asked, to which the Warden, exasperated, said that Sylvia was free to find herself a roommate for next year if that's what she desired.

Sylvia called her mother to say she wanted to leave the college. "I told her it was not the right place for me, and she said, 'you have a good scholarship at Vassar. You need to stay and make the best of it.'" By the next year, she was in a rooming group with classmate Joan Cadden, whose intellectual, politically progressive New York City family more or less adopted her over the next three years.

From then on, Sylvia, who had been an enthusiastic learner in the warm environment of the Quaker Oakwood School, by her own admission maintained a kind of passive aggressive engagement with her academic work. "My attitude was 'I have to be here, but I'm not going to play with you.'" Because she had enjoyed being in theater at Oakwood, Sylvia took drama classes. She remembers a class in which the professor asked the students to leave the room and come back in as if they were entering a ballroom. "I loved that!" she says. "Everyone got to go to the ball!" But after she was cast as a maid in her first production, a senior admonished her. "Don't ever let them put you in another role like that." Everything was complicated, compromised by race. Sylvia understood that, and drama was time consuming, so she moved on to be a history major, with a heavy concentration in political science. "In so many ways, I cut myself off from much that Vassar offered," Sylvia admits. "I don't feel good about that in retrospect."

She had hoped to write her senior thesis on the liberation movements in emerging African countries, but she was discouraged by her history advisor because there was not much literature and research on the subject, and no one on the faculty familiar enough with the subject to judge her work. So, at the last minute, Sylvia switched her major to political science, and decided to write a thesis on the impact of Karl Marx on the philosopher Reinhold Niebuhr. Unaccountably, for such a heady subject, Sylvia said her plan was to just "throw something at the thesis committee." But her new political science advisor, again Wilfred Rumble, took a disillusioned Sylvia in hand, walking her through drafts with the admonition, "Sylvia, you are a bright student and you are going to do this well, and I am going to help you." She looks back on Mr. Rumble with gratitude for taking her seriously and encouraging her to take this last academic task seriously, too. Looking back on her life, Sylvia confesses that the Vassar years were in some ways the most difficult of her life. Now, going back to reunions, she is surprised to meet classmates who also felt somehow inadequate and daunted by their Vassar experience. She had thought she was alone with a feeling of disconnection.

Not so. For Ros Anderson Nesticò, the breastfeeding advocate, and for other classmates, Vassar felt like a stretch. Several of us worried that we might not make it through college. Getting into Vassar was one hurdle. The privilege of being a Vassar girl felt hard earned, and a number of us were not certain that we could pull it off. Getting a Vassar degree was going to require serious application.

"I had the feeling that I didn't know as much as the other girls, that I did not quite fit in," Ros says. "I spent much of my time trying to just stay in college, to conform to what I saw as a model for the Vassar girl. Coming from a small southern city and a public high school background, I always felt pressure to make the grade as far as academics went."

Ros' mother had graduated from the University of Michigan. "My father, who had not gone to college, put great stock in a college education" for his children, Ros says. When she graduated from public high school in Tallahassee, she went north to Vassar. "I wanted a women's college, after my high school experience, where the large classes made it hard for someone introverted to speak up and feel valued. I wanted to be in a school where there would be no male domination in the classroom."

"This was my feeling at the time," Ros says, "though now looking back, if I had to do it over again, I would choose a small liberal arts coeducational college. I hadn't had much experience of the opposite sex and now believe that interacting with men, having to deal with them both in the classroom and out, is definitely part of one's education. It wasn't normal or helpful to encounter the other gender only during a mixer or an occasional weekend at Dartmouth or Yale."

Physical therapist Dorsett Edmonds, too, had a slow start at Vassar, earning C's and wondering if she were really Vassar material. She chose Vassar, where on her admission visit she had seen a girl come racing to class in a raincoat and pajamas, and she thought, "I really like this place!" Her father insisted that the twins attend a women's college, where no boys would distract them, in the east, as opposed to the west, where the atmosphere was too "wild," or the south, where girls' schools, in his opinion, were not serious enough. And he felt that they should attend different colleges.

At the end of her sophomore year, Dorsett went home to Baltimore wondering if she should withdraw and go to nursing school – an idea that received no support at home – and by junior year she hit her stride as a history major. Looking back now, Dorsett points out that the Vassar experience, though challenging, was a fortifying one. "Going to such a good school – and actually graduating – empowered me to feel I had intelligence."

Elizabeth Ratigan's Vassar education, it turns out, gave her the gift of a vocation in the new field of technology. Elizabeth, the computer analyst, had come to Vassar from the suburbs of St. Paul, Minnesota, where she had attended private girls' schools, tested well and earned respectable grades. Elizabeth's mother, Helen, and her Aunt Molly had gone to Vassar. Her Aunt Ruthie, to whom Elizabeth was especially close, had gone to Smith, so that an eastern women's college seemed a natural choice. Her older brother, John, was a student at Dartmouth. In a story similar to that of Ros' father, Elizabeth's father, whose education at Georgetown University had been interrupted when his father died and he was forced to return home to help support his family, was determined that Elizabeth would, like his wife and sisters-in-law, go to one of the Seven Sisters. "His own experience led my father to train his ambitions on his children," she says.

Though most of the students at ophthalmologist Moira Burke's high school were not college bound, she understood that her parents had, Moira says, a "clear expectation" that she would go to college. Her father had even considered that Moira might move beyond what was available at home. "If you don't go to Buffalo State Teacher's College," he said, "you must go to a well-endowed school that will give you a scholarship." When Moira chose Vassar, a New York school that represented an escape from home and her childhood, her aunt was shocked. "How can you do this to your parents," she raged, "going away to school?" Her mother was, in a more passive way, supportive of her goals.

At Vassar, Moira majored in zoology, one of only three members of the Class of '65 to do so, studying fruit flies and taking required pre-med courses in pursuit of her unchanging goal to pursue medicine. Looking back, Moira now says, "Vassar was pivotal. It was the foundation and springboard for my professional life." The college was challenging, though, and sometimes, faced with a difficult course, she feared that she might lose her academic scholarship. To get a sense of exactly how possible her dream was going to be, in her junior year, Moira sat for an early round of medical college admission tests (MCATs) and was reassured when she earned high scores.

I have noted that Vassar students in the Class of '65 were, during our college years, somewhat disengaged from the social revolutions growing in the country, except as interested observers. Dorsett Edmonds, however, was keenly aware of what was happening in the civil rights movement at the time, and angry at herself that she did not have the courage to go to Selma, Alabama, in October 1963, to participate with the Student Nonviolent Coordinating Committee (SNCC) in registering Black voters. A year later, she envied her twin, Mimi, by then at Berkeley, for her involvement with the Free Speech Movement.

While on campus, Sylvia Drew was equally uninvolved. But during the summers, back home in Washington, DC, and in the milieu of Howard University's intellectual cauldron at the epicenter of the civil rights movement, she was swept into social justice activities. In the summer of 1963, the federal department of Health, Education and Welfare (HEW) sent groups of college students, including Sylvia, to Alabama and Mississippi to help enroll students of color in white schools. Parents were asked to sign forms for their children to be eligible for enrollment in white schools. Sylvia and a white student from Columbia were paired and trained to go door to door in Ruleville, Mississippi, introducing the program and inviting families to participate by signing the form. "It was a high-risk decision for parents," Sylvia notes. "Some people lost their houses to arson and their jobs for considering sending their children to white schools. The courage we encountered from those families, living in shotgun shacks in the rural south, who dared to sign the form, was beyond extraordinary."

There was so much in the news to draw our interest from personal and campus issues during our four college years, from 1961 to 1965. With a few exceptions, my friends and I participated in those changes only through discussions in our dormitories, at dinner, or in classrooms. The U.S. sent support troops to Vietnam, beginning in 1961, in a war that would escalate – and be the subject of social unrest – throughout our college years and beyond. By the time we graduated in 1965, most of the men we knew were being drafted to fight in Vietnam or were finding ways to avoid the draft.

The increasingly confrontational events in the civil rights movement spanned most of our four years on campus. In October 1962, James Meredith became the first Black student, under constant guard of federal marshals, to enroll at Ole Miss (the University of Mississippi). This caused a riot on that campus that ended with the intervention of 30,000 federal troops. Riots in Birmingham, Alabama followed in the spring and summer of 1963, culminating in the March on Washington for Jobs and Freedom in August, where Dr. Martin Luther King delivered his "I have a dream" speech in front of the Lincoln Memorial on the Mall. The summer before our senior year, thousands of college students and activists went to southern states to register Black voters, including the boys from the Yale Class of '64, as reported in Howard Gillette's book *Class Divide*. It was an effort surrounded by further violence that would come to be called Freedom Summer. And just before we graduated from Vassar, in March 1965, Martin Luther King, John Lewis, and other civil rights workers led protesters on the famous voting rights march from Selma to Montgomery, Alabama.

Most of us did not get on buses or march on Washington, or find ourselves on the barricades, at least during our college years. That kind of participation would come later, when we had begun to embrace a new sense of ourselves as women and as citizens.

There were two pieces of news that we did feel, personally and viscerally, during our college years. One was the Cuban Missile Crisis in October of 1962. The military stand-off between the U.S. and Russia after the discovery of the nuclear armed Russian missile base in Cuba, just off American shores, would present us with a sobering couple of weeks. Sitting on the floor in someone's room, smoking cigarettes around a communal ashtray, we felt the proximity of world events. Would Kennedy's decision to create a blockade around Cuba stop the Russians, or would we soon be killed in a nuclear war we had feared since childhood? I remember listening to a radio in our room, or someone else's – we all had radios, which served as our principal access to news other than the one television in the basement of Noyes House. After growing up during years of warnings about nuclear winter and dystopian visions of the world after nuclear war, we experienced the Cuban Missile Crisis as an incident that could make it all terrifyingly real. I believed that we could be dead soon, having hardly begun our lives, but I went to class, ate, studied, and did my laundry. And we talked, listened to the radio, worried and talked. The news provided a sobering and enlightening philosophical moment, leading us to contemplate the end of our lives, not to mention the possible end of the world. At the end of 13 days of crisis, President Kennedy announced the deal that would lead Russia to remove the Cuban missile site, and, with a lift in our spirits, we knew we would be saved from nuclear annihilation, at least for the moment. But there was a hum of existential anxiety in the background.

Little more than a year later, on a Friday before Thanksgiving, my dorm mates and I came home from morning classes to eat lunch in the Noyes dining room when the news broke – someone had heard it on the radio – that President Kennedy had been shot in Dallas, Texas. Again, we retreated to our rooms, clustering around radios until the announcer reported that Kennedy had died, and we scattered, each of us to grieve in our own way for the charming young president who seemed uniquely ours, part of a new generation of leaders. I left the dorm and walked around the campus, stunned, passing groups clustered around car windows to hear the news again on the radio. On my way to English class in Rockefeller, I heard that Mr. Bartlett, our professor, weeping, had canceled the class and left the building. That weekend, I had been invited to Yale on a blind date and, as if life *could* go on as usual with the weight of grief we all felt, I went to Yale, semiconscious, for what felt like a strange interlude. On Sunday morning at the Yale law school dorm, someone yelled down the hall that Kennedy's presumed assassin was shot by a Dallas lawyer, Jack Ruby, piling conspiracy upon conspiracy. Back at Vassar on Monday morning, we clustered around the dorm TV to witness the President's small son salute his father's casket as it rolled down the parade route after his funeral. It all felt like a very personal loss.

Though we were not yet marching in the streets, we were not completely out of the social stirrings of the early sixties, however. In freshman year, we were at the center of the storm that was the sexual revolution. And our participation in it came from a surprising source: Vassar President Blanding's infamous sex speech, which took place during the second semester of our freshman year.

It's hard for me to think of formal, proper Sarah Gibson Blanding as a 1930s "radical," as Mrs. Drouilhet remembered her in the *Vassar Encyclopedia*, or as "a woman with a pro-Roosevelt 'liberal' cult of influential people," as one unhappy alumna described her. These retrospective descriptions put a new spin on the iconic event of our college years – President Blanding's speech to the entire student body in April 1962. With the passage of women's suffrage in 1920, political engagement was fair game for women, including these "30s radicals," as Mrs. Drouilhet and Miss Blanding, who had apparently participated as emancipated women in the political life of that era. Their view of sex was more, or maybe less, complicated.

On April 4, 1962, Miss Blanding announced to some 1,530 Vassar students, assembled in the college chapel for an all-college convocation that "decent girls, Vassar girls, don't have sex before marriage. Students who chose to engage in premarital sex," she said, "should think about withdrawing from the college."

That particular gathering had begun with the unwelcome news that the next year's tuition would increase from $2,500 to $2,800 per year – news that worried me on my parents' behalf. I was startled, then, when Miss Blanding went on, without preamble, to talk about sex. Few of us, raised in the moral environment of the 1950s, in our knee socks, pleated skirts and Shetland sweaters, would have found her message in conflict with what we had been hearing from adults all our lives. Nor could we have predicted the shock that lecture generated, on campus and beyond, in the spring of 1962. It was to have the effect of an earthquake on the Vassar campus over the next week.

Whether or not we adhered to the idea, it was a given for our generation of girls that we had to save our virginity for the marriage bed. Girls who had sex before marriage were branded and girls who became pregnant "out of wedlock" were the subject of scandal. You could do almost everything else, but actual sexual intercourse was only for the very brave or the very careless. For some, just a generation later, that idea was preposterously old fashioned, and sexual experimentation had become a rite of passage in adolescence. What happened at Vassar that spring must seem laughable to young women now. It was a paradigm shifting moment for naïve me.

Because Miss Blanding's message was so familiar to me, so often repeated in my childhood, I didn't at first sense the rage building up in the chapel, which would soon spread into every dormitory living room on campus. I had no idea of the tempest I would step into back at Noyes House, where a clutch of freshmen, sophomores, and juniors gathered to discuss the talk (seniors then lived together in Main Building). "It's an outrage," shouted one student. "It's none of her business," said another. It was? It wasn't? Where had I been? By the end of that enlightening evening, I knew a great deal more about where to find contraceptives and how to get an illegal abortion (in a pre-Roe v. Wade world) in Poughkeepsie. I now know from post college class surveys that some 30 percent of my classmates had already been sexually active. Was it privilege that allowed girls to be more comfortable and adventurous with sex, or was I particularly naïve and inexperienced?

The following week, the student newspaper, the *Vassar Miscellany News* (the *Misc*) took the unusual step of publishing – with "no outside circulation" – a supplement to its weekly edition that both the student newspaper and the administration felt "of value and importance only to the Vassar community" (not true as it turned out). The supplement, an extra-budget publication, could be purchased for 10 cents a copy on campus. It reported on a survey that the *Misc* and the *Comment*, another student publication, had distributed asking several questions about students' response to Miss Blanding's speech. Of the 1,040 students who participated in the survey (almost two-thirds of the student body), slightly more than half agreed with Miss Blanding's moral position.

Said one student in support of chastity, "this college would not be respected if it did not take a stand for the dignity of young women ... premarital relations do not signify personal freedom." In retrospect, this sentiment has a feminist ring to it. One alumna, taking a feminist point of view, thought that, "To women who were educated in the lingering shadow of the great feminists [of the first wave of feminism in the early twentieth century], the tolerance of many college girls for indecent behavior – and also their pursuit of early marriage, however decent – represent surrender to masculine standards and masculine dominance." In the age of "#me too" rejection of sexually aggressive behavior in men, this sentiment has the ring of truth, but it didn't to us then.

Taking up Miss Blanding's view, Betty Friedan wrote in the notes section of *The Feminine Mystique*, "The real question for the educator would seem to me to be whether these girls were getting from their education the serious lifetime goals only education can give them. If they are, they can be trusted to be responsible for their sexual behavior. President Blanding indeed defied the mystique to say boldly that if girls are not in college for education, they should not be there at all." I have spent the greater part of the last 60 or so years thinking of Miss Blanding's speech as retrogressive, informed by the mores of the 1950s. Many students were influenced by the "liberating" idea that sexual activity was a matter of personal choice, not moral dictates of the culture, while Friedan – and perhaps Miss Blanding – saw the pursuit of sexual engagement as a diversion from the serious purpose of education, the source of real empowerment for women. What we heard from the speech was "Be a good girl or leave." Maybe the message really was "Be a serious student or leave," though that message still assumes that it was not possible to be both a serious student and sexually active – an assumption not made about boys.

Those students who objected to the speech expressed resentment that Vassar, a "liberal" arts institution that prided itself on the development of individual responsibility and critical thinking, felt that it could not trust students to use their own judgment about their private lives. Said one, "Vassar no longer stands for the freedom of each student to define her own moral code and to conduct her private life within a set of social relations." One student opined that if chastity was to be a requirement for Vassar students, if the college was to become the "Poughkeepsie Victorian Seminary for Young Virgins," then it should be explicitly stated in the admissions materials. She added that the student body might be a lot less interesting in the future. Everyone was shocked at Miss Blanding's assertion that those who had premarital sex should withdraw from the college; two respondents said they planned to leave the school. The campus debate on sex was inevitably the subject of late-night discussions, more candid than any I'd had back in Philadelphia.

A month went by and the sex speech tempest was beginning to die down on campus when, in early May, the *New York Herald-Tribune* broke the story after a copy of the *Misc* supplement "became available," as the *Trib* put it. Overnight, Vassar's news became national news as newspapers across the country, from Seattle to Rochester, carried stories on Miss Blanding's speech and the ensuing "uproar" at the school. The press had a field day with the headlines: "The Idea! Say the Vassar Girls" (*New York Post*), "Vassar Scolds Wild Students" (*Louisville Courier-Journal*), "The Tizzy at Vassar" (*Hartford Courant*), and "Sex Hex Vexes Vassar" (*Boston Herald*).

The part of the story that shocked readers was not that 52 percent of Vassar students supported Miss Blanding (a finding that would be incomprehensible to contemporary students), but that 48 percent of the students – including eight percent who were undecided – *did not* support her. Some editorials speculated that boys would come to date Vassar girls for the "wrong reasons," others that Vassar girls were "male starved desperate females." Everyone had a theory about who was to blame for the moral decline among American youth – especially Vassar girls. Some thought college girls were at risk because they postponed marriage until after college, and were trained to think for themselves with no means for gaining experience. Professors teaching the "fashion of the times" allowed the girls to think they could "create standards according to their own whim."

Soon the Vassar story had a global audience, further illustrating the gulf between attitudes toward sex then and now. The Vassar library archives contain clippings of coverage in Italian and French newspapers along with one from the Chinese language *China Tribune* in New York City. The *London Sunday Times* commented wryly that "Students in American colleges think they have a right to do anything except join the Communist Party." Eleanor Roosevelt in her syndicated column warned that "Freedom is a natural demand of youth, but it does require preparation." Margaret Mead stepped into the conversation in a *Redbook Magazine* piece, noting that the "central issue about premarital sex relations is the risk of producing illegitimate children – children who from the start are denied the protection every human society has found it necessary to give."

Our cohorts at other colleges weighed in with their own perspectives on premarital sex. A *Washington Post* survey of students at Columbia, Cornell, Harvard, Princeton, Wesleyan and Yale (interestingly, it did not survey women's colleges) yielded the majority opinion that matters of sex "are a student's private business." Berkeley's *Daily Californian* added that sexual experimentation was okay for boys but not for girls. The *Cornell Sun* speculated that the speech was made to "pacify alumnae and those parents who do not have much faith in the maturity of their daughters." Novelist and sports writer, Frank Deford, then a senior at Princeton, wrote a send-up of the Vassar story, a one-scene play entitled "Miss Blanding Builds Her Dream Girl" for the Princeton student newspaper.

Miss Blanding received a flood of fan mail from parents and alumnae. In subsequent interviews, including an article in the November 1962 issue of *McCall's Magazine* titled "The Day I Spoke Off the Cuff to the Girls of Vassar," Blanding referred to the number of magazine articles tending to promote promiscuity. Perhaps she was reacting to the work of Helen Gurley Brown, whose book *Sex and the Single Girl* would be published that year, 1962, and who was already promoting her brand of feminism (defined by freedom of sexual expression) for single girls in the "Cosmo girl" archetype of her magazine, *Cosmopolitan.* Though Brown's writing would be directed to single working women, not necessarily college educated women, *Sex and the Single Girl* would capture the culture's loosening view of sex – something we too were feeling.

I think one effect all the news coverage had on us, other than giving the administration headaches, was that we came to believe that as Vassar students, we were news. When the company that produced the movie "Easy Rider" decided to try it out at the Juliet Theatre, just off campus, and then annoyingly (and incorrectly) reported in the *New York Times* that the Vassar girls had cooed and squealed over it in their knee socks and kilts, we saw the dark side of notoriety. When *The Times* displayed a large photo of a coed touch football game on the Vassar quad in the Sunday Sports section one fall, we gave it a celebrity shrug.

Though the Fundies story and Miss Blanding's speech were unrelated, both strike me as examples of values about women that would soon go out of style.

Sarah Gibson Blanding retired as president of Vassar in June 1964, at the end of our junior year. Her successor, Alan Simpson, noted in a speech at his inaugural ceremony in October of that year that he understood (perhaps better than we did) that the college was shepherding Vassar students on a trajectory that would take women to a new place in American culture. "We are still in the midst of an unfinished revolution in the status of women," he said. It was in its infancy when Vassar opened; in its adolescence with the suffragettes. It will be in its maturity a century or so from now ... It is a revolution which has shattered the old image – of the man striding forward to conquer while the woman trudges behind with the baby in her arms – without replacing it with a new one. And it leaves, like all revolutions, a trail of frustration in its wake."

It was an accurate and prescient introduction to the world we would enter in just a few months. But he offered further comfort as we passed through Taylor Gate into that world: "It is not a choice of marriage or a career, or of marriage and a career, but of a life lived in phases, each with its opportunities for fulfillment." And so it was.

CHAPTER 5

Changing the World – the Sixties

"As the sixties unfolded, we got the idea that we could have an impact on the world, that we could change things ..."
From the Bank Street conversations

T he first reunion book for the Class of '65, published in 1969, reports that eight of us had spent two years in the Peace Corps, posted to Africa, Asia, and South America, in a volunteer program conceived by President Kennedy and authorized by Congress just as we matriculated at Vassar in September 1961. It was a life altering experience for the young Americans who volunteered to provide support to schools, social and economic development, governments, agriculture and the environment.

In 1969, just four years out of college, 245 (out of 364 graduates) had married, and there were a number of babies. At the same time about 50 of us had earned graduate degrees and another 20 were working toward further degrees. Six of us had become lawyers and we had two newly trained physicians. We were walking through any doors that would open for us.

Change was already upon us in the summer of 1965, for everyone, including those of our classmates who, with relief, were flashing engagement rings in the cafeteria line senior year, whose weddings filled social calendars all that summer.

But what about the rest of us, who now really needed to start defining ourselves and our place in the world as individuals, outside the conveniently defining role of wife? What did we do? In the summer of 1965, I prepared myself for my first "real" job by learning to speed type and taking dictation at the Philadelphia School of Office Training, because a mere college education was not going to get a young woman an office job. Ros Anderson Nesticò spent the summer traveling in Italy with her mother, before deciding to stay there to study Italian language. Moira Burke was poised to go to medical school. Dede Thompson Bartlett, longing to return to Paris, where she had spent her junior year in college, hung around New York, going to a lot of parties but unable to find a good job. "My life was aimless," Dede says. Seeking to help her daughter find focus and structure, her mother took her down to NYU, which at the time did not require graduate records exams, and on the spot, Dede enrolled in a master's degree program in American history.

When intrepid Hope Oliker Hageman graduated from Vassar in 1965, she spent the summer working as a reporter for a daily newspaper in upstate New York, saving money to buy a plane ticket to Central Africa to marry Alvin Hageman. Hope and Alvin had known each other since childhood in Auburn, New York, and they were remotely connected by the fact that their younger brothers were friends. One summer while they were still in college, the brothers fixed them up, and by the end of the summer, they were a couple. Upon graduation, Alvin was accepted into the Peace Corps, destined for the new African country of Malawi, established just a year earlier, in 1964. There, he would work as an accountant for a cotton marketing cooperative. While Hope was at Vassar for her senior year, Alvin trained at Syracuse University, learning a Bantu dialect and the Kalamazoo accounting system to prepare for his assignment. When Hope graduated, Alvin was already in Malawi. There, over their parents' objections, they would marry. "My parents weren't happy," Hope says. "They thought we were too young. 'How can you do this to that poor boy?' my father asked. But I was very headstrong, and they knew I was going to go, so there wasn't much point arguing with me." At the end of the summer, Hope flew to Central Africa with a wedding dress, made by a neighbor in Auburn, in her suitcase.

Sheltered as we had been in the academic environment at Vassar, most of us were not the first people to join the social unrest bubbling to the surface in the country in 1965. But as the decade moved along, *everything,* every expectation, every institution became unmoored. Few certainties, few assumptions were left unchallenged. "The late 1960s was one of the most divisive periods in American history," says Robert Brigham, professor of history and international relations at Vassar, in the Fall 2019 *Vassar Quarterly.* "Not since the Civil War had the social fabric of the country been so torn."

Brigham captures in cameo the atmosphere of the world we entered that June, summarizing the issues and challenges before us: the war in Vietnam, which by the end of 1968 had resulted in 27 million young men drafted for war, and 35,000 deaths; the civil rights movement, with both peaceful protests and violent eruptions following the assassination of Dr. King; women "tired of the patriarchal nature of many anti-war groups;" rough treatment by police responding to protests;

bonfires igniting draft cards and bras; psychedelic drugs; the 1968 Democratic National Convention, disrupted by political violence in the streets of Chicago. Then there was the sexual revolution, the frustration at the slow pace of change, the "generation gap." And in another effort to assure equal access to institutions, many single sex colleges and universities moved to coeducation – including Vassar, which began admitting men in 1969.

The Vietnam War, which many Americans saw as an imperialist power grab in Asia, was at the center of many anti-war protests. A number of the women I interviewed reported that they had participated in demonstrations against the Vietnam War on the streets of Boston, New York and Washington in the mid-to-late 1960s. Debbie Michaelson Kolb, now living in Boston, spent weekends demonstrating against the war with her future husband, Jonathan, while working in her first job in Harvard's economics department. In Washington, DC, Elizabeth Ratigan, newly trained as a computer programmer – a new field in 1965 – also demonstrated against the war, even as she worked at the Institute for Defense Analysis (IDA), a military research program funded by academic institutions and targeted by anti-war demonstrators. By 1968, IDA would be a target of the anti-war movement that erupted on the Columbia University campus, just after Dr. King's assassination and the ensuing violence in neighboring Harlem. The unrest lasted more than a week before police were called in to break up the student protests. Ultimately, it achieved at least one of the results the students wanted: the university cut its ties with IDA, which they believed was "directly supplying research on war materiel for the war in Vietnam."

Dorsett Edmunds, who was just beginning to live her mission to make the world a better place, had her own experience with the social conflict created by the Vietnam

War. While Dorsett, a Peace Corps volunteer (PCV), was in the mountains of Kenya, teaching, she heard that the CIA had infiltrated the Corps in Thailand in 1967, in support of the U.S. government's political efforts on behalf of the Vietnam War. It could have been a rumor started by anti-Americans, but a Kenyan Member of Parliament seemed to confirm the report. The Minister was visibly upset, hurt, and angry at the idea of CIA involvement in the Peace Corps. Was the U.S. perhaps intending to use the Peace Corps as cover for supporting the war? It was all very disturbing to the volunteers, who felt used by the government, their hard work manipulated to counter-balance an imperialist world view of the U.S. They asked each other, Dorsett says, "Are we now Marines in velvet gloves? Damn you, America, for polluting what is good!" Even the students in Dorsett's classroom were confused, one 16-year-old girl asking her, "Why are the Americans fighting a war 8,000 kilometers away? We understand fighting people who steal our cattle ... what is America doing there?" "I couldn't answer her question," Dorsett says. "I was stumped."

Dorsett and other Peace Corps volunteers prepared a letter objecting to the Vietnam War, to be sent to the *New York Times*, but when the local Peace Corps office got wind of it, Dorsett and her colleagues were told that they would be acting against the policies of the Peace Corps and the volunteers, who were to be "apolitical." "What we all understood, though," Dorsett says, "is that we *were* part of the political fabric of the U.S. government."

Meanwhile, other classmates went to the barricades for other festering issues of the age. In 1963, unlike most of us, before we were out of school, Mattie Brody Banshaf, later leader of an activist women's singing group, and Caroline Morris, who became a lawyer, had marched on Washington in 1963 with Martin Luther King Jr. Martha Burke-Hennessey, who would become a movie executive; Ruth Eller, who would become an Episcopal priest; and Susan Perry, an artist and photographer, marched for civil rights and women's issues, as did Enid Rubenstein, a lawyer, for health care and fair employment practices for women.

Sylvia Drew Ivie's 1964 summer in Ruleville, Mississippi, registering Black students for white schools, had already put her at the center of the civil rights movement. That experience gave Sylvia her introduction to a voting rights activist who would soon become a household name in the country. She and her co-worker, a white student from Columbia University, knocked on the door of Fanny Lou Hamer, a resident of Ruleville, who with much scowling and growling at these college students, nevertheless signed the enrollment form for her adopted children to attend white schools. She had had to adopt her children because a white doctor had given her a hysterectomy without her consent – a forced sterilization so common it was dubbed a "Mississippi appendectomy." A year after Sylvia's visit, Hamer, whose civil rights work was focused on registering Blacks to vote, co-founded the Mississippi Freedom Democratic Party (MFDP), challenging the Mississippi Democratic Party's efforts to keep Black citizens from voting. That summer she took an MFDP delegation to the Democratic National Convention in Atlantic City, New Jersey, demanding that they be recognized. While at the convention, she delivered a passionate, blistering speech about racial prejudice in the south that was later televised for a national audience, making her a household name.

Sylvia's encounter with Hamer was serendipitous, but that same summer, she would meet and come under the influence of Dr. William Montague Cobb, who would introduce her to the issue that would define her career – equal access to health care for people of color. To start that career, as Sylvia thought about it, the law began to emerge as "the right tool for the moment." Though she had been accepted to the law schools at both Harvard and Howard University, she chose Howard, where she found intellectual thought filtered through a racial lens. "At Howard, I was at the center of civil rights law theory, and we were all called upon to be a part of the struggle," she says. "It felt like the right place to be."

Classmate Susan Gordon Lydon narrates her own experience of the turbulent 1960s and '70s in her moving memoir *Take the Long Way Home,* published in 1993. In her book, Susan tells the story of life as a journalist in the avant-garde of the publishing world in that era. She was writing for the *Village Voice, Ramparts* and *Rolling Stone,* of which she was a founding writer and editor, along with her husband Michael Lydon and publisher Jann Wenner. Often feeling marginalized by the men, including her husband, while working with them to create the publication, Susan became increasingly radicalized as a feminist, in her writing and in the company she sought in women's consciousness raising groups. Her article "The Politics of Orgasm," published in *Ramparts* and later anthologized in feminist Robin Morgan's collection of writings from the women's movement, *Sisterhood is Powerful,* made Susan an important feminist voice of the era, one of the "midwives" our class would produce. In the article, she challenged the prevailing Freudian idea that women's orgasms were only "real" if they were experienced vaginally, and that the women who did not have that experience were frigid, making them once again inferior to men, even in bed. Susan's memoir would go on to describe her descent into more than two decades of drug addiction and, briefly, life as a junkie on the streets of Manhattan, among other mean streets, until she found her way to recovery in her forties. This was yet another tale of the era, the drug culture that wove itself, sometimes dangerously, into its dominant social movements.

Classmate Mollie Ramsey Foster spent her first year after graduation with her husband, Terry, on the Berkeley campus of the University of California. The Free Speech Movement had, since the fall of 1964, upended campus life at Berkeley, challenging campus authorities and making alarming headlines across the country. Newly married, Mollie and Terry were pursuing graduate studies at Berkeley, Mollie studying to earn a California teaching credential.

The Free Speech Movement had its origins in Freedom Summer 1964 when Berkeley students joined those from Yale and other colleges across the country to travel to Mississippi to register African Americans to vote. Coming back to the Berkeley campus the following fall committed to civil rights and opposition to the Vietnam War, students began to rally in support of those political causes. University rules forbidding political activity on campus, however, silenced them. Tensions escalated and students began to demonstrate for "free speech" on campus. The university ultimately gave in to student demands for political expression. Subsequent sit-ins and other activities marked the beginning of an era of civil disobedience across the country in support of the two principal political movements of the 1960s, against racism and American imperialism in the world.

The following year, the Free Speech Movement was still going strong. "Two or three days a week, I would go over to Sproul Hall at lunchtime," Mollie remembers, "to hear political speeches by Mario Savio, the principal student spokesman for the movement." Watching the milling crowd of students, some lounging on the steps, some tossing their long hair to the side as they raised fists, Mollie soaked up the energy, the political passion in the air on that sunny California campus that fall. Mollie, who had grown up in a politically active family in Omaha, Nebraska, describes her parents as "idealists, dreamers" who cared deeply about progressive politics, civil rights, the arts and education. While Mr. Ramsey, a lawyer and banker, was deeply immersed in the Urban League, Mrs.

Ramsey had served for eight years on the Omaha School Board, where she was influential in getting the school system to hire its first African American teacher. Mollie had found Vassar to be a community "sheltered" from political activism. Berkeley and the Free Speech Movement constituted an awakening for her, clarifying her concerns about the war and about social justice. The experience left Mollie feeling a gulf between her own priorities and what she imagined as the "Junior League" approach to social change in which some of her college friends now found themselves. The Junior League, a women's volunteer network in cities around the country, has for over a century involved itself in undeniably important work on a number of social issues. At the same time, membership in the League promised access to a network that could be socially advantageous. It was, our mothers said, "a good way to meet other nice women in a new city," which gave its work a kind of "noblesse oblige" feel.

We all felt the impact of the 1960s social revolutions. Of the eight women who shared accounts of their lives with me, Dorsett Edmunds and Sylvia Drew told stories that particularly and uniquely exemplified the impact of that time, and those revolutions, on their lives as they unfolded.

The Physical Therapist: Dorsett's Story

Because of her personality and interests, Dorsett Edmunds absorbed the ethos of the sixties and, by embracing the values of the era, became a beacon of change, a woman who is still working at the head of progressive movements.

"I have always been interested in personal freedom," Dorsett says, "and empowerment of all kinds, in work that supports marginalized people." Dorsett, a small trim woman with a radiant smile and a shock of white striping through still dark brown hair, wears brightly colored scarves suggesting the Native American and Hispanic American culture of the southwest. She has the weathered skin of a lifetime outdoors and a youthful spirit, her eyes bright and alert and her face animated with energy.

On the day I called to arrange a phone interview with Dorsett, who lives in Tucson, Arizona, I caught her in the middle of a very busy Sunday schedule. Her day had started at Southside Presbyterian Church, where she holds a leadership position as the "worship elder." The church, a sanctuary for refugees and asylum seekers in this city on the border with Mexico, has for many years attracted activists – Catholics, Presbyterians, Buddhists, Jews – who care about the plight of refugees from war torn and crime-ridden central American countries. After the service and a meeting on the worship budget, Dorsett went to her Sunday soccer game. At 76 then, the oldest team member by at least 15 years, she was a fullback in the Tucson Women's Soccer League. That Sunday would end at the theater – for an original play, "Sanctuary," about the beginning of the sanctuary movement in Tucson, put on by the Borderlands Theatre Group. I found time to talk to her on another day.

Dorsett grew up in the suburbs of Baltimore, Maryland, with her identical twin sister, Mimi, two adorable little girls with big eyes and brown wavy hair. The Edmunds family, including a younger sister and brother, lived in a converted Mennonite meeting house on a farm, surrounded by cows, ducks, two dogs, a pig named Emma and a goat named Phoebe. The girls had a traditional Catholic childhood in the Green Spring Valley and were educated at Bryn Mawr School, a nondenominational private girls' school. Later Dorsett would find herself in a life she defines as "dominated by service" – driven to effect positive change in the world – teaching in Kenya, marching on Washington against the

Vietnam War and for civil rights, even briefly joining a Maoist community. Her life took her far from Baltimore and the traditional world in which she grew up.

Dorsett had been a serious student at Bryn Mawr. "My twin sister, Mimi, was the more outgoing of the two of us, the one who could laugh, be happy and fun loving," Dorsett says. "In class, I sat in the middle of the room, my attention on the teacher. Mimi was always in the back, talking with her desk mate. I would think 'why can't I be that way, too?'" Dorsett says that among twins, birth order often confers a kind of status to the first born. "We were always 'Mimi Dorsett,' not the reverse. Mimi was the first born, and I never lost the feeling that as a second born twin, I was less important or powerful," Dorsett says.

Mimi dated more, had been given the ultimate status symbol, a scarf from the local boys' school. Dorsett, more cerebral and less self-confident, never felt entirely secure in her environment. She attributes her feeling of kinship with marginalized populations to her sense of being on the margin in her own life. "I wasn't interested in being a debutante, or joining the Junior League," she says. Feeling on the outer edges of her family, she had different ideas. "I thought of becoming a nun."

She was reaching for community herself. Dorsett shares two significant stories from her adolescence that helped define her world view. Aware of racial issues in Baltimore and the suburbs – hearing about demonstrations against the segregation of local pools and parks – Dorsett went to a Quaker conference at Buck Hill Falls, Pennsylvania, where she participated in sessions focused on peacemaking, nonviolence, and civil rights. Later, as president of the Christian Association at Bryn Mawr School, Dorsett was responsible for scheduling speakers at the Friday assembly. She lined up a series of speakers – a rabbi, a Quaker, representatives of eastern religions, to bring new voices to the school. "I was on the honor role, a good athlete, I got academic and citizenship awards, but still I felt inadequate," Dorsett muses.

Partly on the basis of her visit to the campus – with the girl in pajamas and a raincoat, and the campus informality that communicated – she chose Vassar. Mimi went to Bradford Junior College, finishing her education, as it happens, at the University of California at Berkeley, Mr. Edmunds having by that time given up his argument against western schools.

Dorsett, after a shaky start, learned how to thrive at Vassar, and to appreciate the gifts it gave her. She had not participated, so far, in the civil rights movement, as she had yearned to do. But, taking a shower in the fall of her senior year, warm water streaming down around her, Dorsett thought about how lucky we were in our world, with all our access to water and shelter and food. She thought about what she would do after college. "I have been given so much," she thought, "and I want to give back. Perhaps the Peace Corps – doing work in another culture ..." She adds now that volunteering for the Peace Corps was a way of "not feeling like a failure," at a moment when she had no career objectives and no husband in the offing. Her father had advised her to get a job as a secretary to a really good boss, but she thought, "No, if I get a job, I'd rather be writing the letters, not typing them."

"Now I wanted to reach out to new experience," she says. Dorsett had been hearing about the Peace Corps, a Kennedy initiative approved by Congress in the fall of our freshman year to "promote world peace and friendship," and as a response to criticism of U.S. "imperialism." The program had been training volunteers since the summer of 1962, so Dorsett and seven other members of the Class of '65 were part of only the fourth corps of volunteers to be sent to work in rural communities around the world.

She took the Peace Corps test in November of senior year,

and later discovered that in one of those freaky twin coincidences, her sister Mimi had taken the same test on the same day at Berkeley. Without consulting each other, they had both decided to join the Peace Corps, and in another twist of fate, both were sent to Kenya after the Peace Corps figured out that there really were two Edmunds girls with the same face applying to be volunteers, and not just duplicate applications. Though they were sent to different regions, the twins were able to see each other occasionally.

Dorsett spent her two years in the Peace Corps teaching at Katkenda Girls High School. A mountain bush school, it had just opened at the initiative of Kenya's President Jomo Kenyatta, who was the first Kenyan leader interested in educating girls beyond elementary school. Dorsett joined another Peace Corps volunteer, two Kenyan teachers and a principal in the school's inaugural year, teaching a variety of subjects to 25 girls. By the end of her second year there, the school had 35 girls enrolled, and three had earned a high school diploma.

More than 50 years later, Dorsett looks back with pride, defining her experience as that of a midwife to the school, a part of the beginning of girls' education in Kenya. Wanting to see what happened to the school in the half century since she was there, Dorsett went back in 2017, accompanied by her sister Mimi and her son Gabe, to find that the school now had 860 students, new buildings, and at least one graduate who became Minister of Education. Dressed by the community in traditional robes, Dorsett gave the school an album of her photos from 50 years before, and spoke at a joyous reception in her honor, attended by 950 people. "I told them I felt so honored to have been a part of the school's successful early history," she says.

In 1968, Dorsett came home to New York City and to a country more turbulent than the one she had left. Re-entry was not easy after such a life altering experience, and Dorsett had had a taste of radical politics. She began to connect with other returned Peace Corps Volunteers. As classmate Joy Miller Frechtling notes in a reunion piece on Dorsett, "Returning from the intense experience of living among the poor and uneducated in Africa, the PCVs mobilized in protest against Apartheid in South Africa and Gulf Oil investments in Mozambique, Angola, and Guinea Bissau." Participating in public demonstrations against Gulf Oil and "American imperialism in other countries," Dorsett appeared in a photo of one demonstration, with a New York radical group on the front business page of the *Wall Street Journal*. She then went home to Baltimore for the weekend, carrying copies of the *Journal* which she left in the hall. They caught her father's eye, and the next morning, after burning the newspapers in the back yard, he told Dorsett, "You can leave this house and do not come back." Dorsett remembers standing at the front door tearfully shouting at her father that she would come see her mother any time she wanted, but in reality, her father's sentiments cemented the fact that in so many ways, she had moved away from her childhood. Some years later, at her sister's wedding, her father, now separated from her mother, invited Dorsett for a talk. "I don't agree with you, but I understand your point of view," he said, and they reconciled.

After her time in Africa, Dorsett enrolled in graduate school at Columbia University in a program that gave Peace Corps returnees nine graduate credits toward a master's degree in teaching, while she student-taught in a Brownsville, Queens, public school. "Graduate school was an easy transition," Dorsett says, "and a good thing to do."

However, student teaching in a hostile school environment was anything but easy. The girls at the high school in Kenya had been excited and engaged in their schoolwork. Instead of being eager to learn, as the Kenyan girls were, Brownsville students were often defeated, discouraged by the systemic indifference to their circumstances, and disaffected from school. Brownsville was the site of much community activism, and the school system was rife with conflict with the "white establishment." Discipline was a chronic issue, and the cultural divide between urban Black students and a young white female teacher felt nearly impossible for her to surmount, even as culturally practiced as she had become.

But Dorsett persisted in fighting against what she considered to be unfair practices – this time taking on standardized testing on behalf of her Brownsville students. "My students were required to take tests on which they were unprepared to do well," Dorsett explains. She believed that the students were meant to fail the tests, so that the school would qualify for more federal aid, "and the experience of failure was demoralizing for the kids. I stood up at a teacher's meeting to object to the tests, saying they were too hard for the kids, and the next day I found a pink slip in my mailbox." Dorsett went to the teacher's union representative for help, but he suggested she would be better off teaching somewhere else. He felt, he said, that given the environment, it was probably the wrong time for a white female teacher to be in the school.

It was during those years Dorsett was at Columbia earning a master's degree that the campus erupted in student revolts. In April 1968, students launched a campaign against the war and military drafts. This happened just a few weeks after Martin Luther King was assassinated; just after President Lyndon Johnson announced he would not run for re-election, surprising the nation; and shortly after the Americans' launch of the deadly Tet Offensive escalated the war in Vietnam. Unrest was fueled by psychedelic drugs, rock music, and political, racial, cultural, and sexual causes, and organized by radical student groups like the Students for a Democratic Society (SDS).

Dorsett was not involved in the Columbia protests. While getting her teaching credential, she also worked as an assistant to a professor of African Studies at Columbia, helping to edit anthologies of African history and literature, and a magazine of intercultural education. In the fall of 1969, acting against the wishes of her boss, Dorsett went to Washington, DC to join a half million women on the Mall in a demonstration against military intervention in Vietnam. She remembers riot police teargassing demonstrators, while she and others ran to harbor in a gas station. Such was the tenor of the times, with Dorsett in the thick of it all.

Moving into her mid-twenties, Dorsett thought of the advice given her by a friend of her father, who warned her that it was okay for a "girl" to be unmarried until she was 26, but after that the door to marriage would close and she would in all probability be an old maid. Most of her social circle were East Africans or African Americans, who were all working to support the Black Panthers. With two other white women who had been in the Peace Corps and with her own brand of fearless dedication, she joined the Panthers at the African Cultural Arts Festival in Algeria, sleeping under a desert sky. "I was so involved in what I was doing that I wasn't so interested in being in a romantic relationship," Dorsett says. "We believed we were changing the world for the better. We felt important, with or without marriage and children."

"But were we too fringy?" she wonders, looking back. She admits that even then, she felt some conflict about her choices, a part of her still seeking the approval of her father, and wishing for positive social judgment. Dorsett supplies an example of the conflict we all felt to some extent – a wish to break out of the social rigidity of our childhoods in the 1950s, and still an unshakable yearning for the social acceptability our parents wanted, through us and for us.

Through her political activities, Dorsett became involved with, and eventually lived in a commune whose leader identified himself as a Maoist. This would become her family for a while – a family composed of one couple with two children, Jim, the Maoist intellectual, and three women, including Dorsett. Reflecting on it now, Dorsett recalls that the commune was dominated by the men, who expected the women to manage the home and the children. Realizing that they felt like second class citizens in the commune – as opposed to the Peace Corps, where they felt they had equal voices – Dorsett and the other women began to focus on women's issues, reading Simone de Beauvoir and Gloria Steinem. They began to meet as a consciousness raising group, exploring how they felt about themselves as women, encouraging each other to speak out. "The experience woke me up to what relationships could be like."

Eventually the Maoist group made a communal decision to leave New York. Meeting for several weeks, they identified Charlotte, North Carolina, a city with growing industry in the south, which appealed to them, and with the presence of a university that gave the community intellectual heft. Jim and the others imagined that Charlotte would be a good place to organize workers "for the revolution," in which capitalism would be crushed.

Once in Charlotte, Dorsett began to find the commune's political climate too rigid, and soon she moved with the other two women to found the Charlotte Women's Center, which, she says, "became a hub of women's work for self-determination and definition." There, with the Helen Reddy anthem "I am Woman" in their ears, Dorsett and three other women leaders started consciousness raising groups and other empowering activities for women. Dorsett was named to a Commission on the Status of Women in Charlotte. Eventually, the Women's Center fell into a heated divide. Two of the women, who had become lovers, wanted the center to focus on lesbian issues, while Dorsett and the fourth woman, who were straight, found the evolving focus too angry and too anti-male. "I didn't want to hate men," Dorsett says. She was at the time involved in one of the important relationships of her adult life with a man she had met in Charlotte. That romance eventually ended.

At the same time, newly armed with a master's degree in education in curriculum development, Dorsett applied for a teaching position at Central Piedmont Community College. She hoped to teach African American history and literature, and the English department chair hired her on the spot. "I was learning a lot about women and society then," she says. With the support of a colleague and mentor who admired her work, and no doubt her spirit, she developed a women's studies course. After writing a series of position papers on feminist issues, published in the *Charlotte Observer*, Dorsett was named to the faculty senate at the college, where she chaired its Committee on Sexism in the Curriculum. "I never saw myself as a radical feminist, but I began to be viewed as one by colleagues at the college!" Dorsett says. "'Don't try to be Jane Fonda here,' some said," and one colleague, a chemist whose wife was a biologist and a friend of Dorsett's, warned her, "You cut it out, don't corrupt my wife."

In 1980, after 10 years in Charlotte, the breakup of a relationship and the suicide of a good friend upset the balance in Dorsett's life, and she sought a new challenge. Her sister Mimi, then a producer for anchor Ed Bradley at CBS's "60 Minutes," had produced a story on Vision Quest, an outdoor program based in Tucson, Arizona. Using old fashioned wagon trains to give troubled adolescents an alternative to detention and a new start through hard work and outdoor adventure, Vision Quest made cross country trips with teenagers assigned to the program by the courts. The teens applied themselves to hard work managing and repairing the wagons, doing carpentry and other necessary jobs to keep the wagon train going, and finding their way back from crime and a downward spiral. "Go to Tucson," Mimi said.

"I had come to understand that the political is personal and the personal is political," Dorsett says. "Our personal lives are connected to the social fabric, and I began to move from the larger political movements to the more personal of choices, identity, well-being, and service." Dorsett got a job with Vision Quest, serving as a scout, finding camping spots for the wagons, mules, horses, and equipment along the way. One of those stops, and her first coup, was a camp on the Washington Mall, in front of the Lincoln Memorial, where the group had arrived for a lobbying visit to senators and congressmen to gain support of the program in the U.S. court system.

The personal, one-on-one contact with the teenagers helped lift the sadness she felt from the dual losses of her friend and the romance. It reminded her of the power of healing in individual work. After three years with the program, Dorsett, now almost 40, began to think about formal education for a future as a healer. Using her growing sense of self and imagining a grand leap into a new direction, she applied to both medical school and a graduate program in physical therapy at Hahnemann Hospital in Philadelphia, Pennsylvania. She was admitted to both and, after some reflection, chose to get a degree in physical therapy. In the reunion interview by Joy Frechtling, Dorsett explains, "I chose physical therapy because I was interested in the intersection of science and movement. Doctors work mostly with drugs and knives and have a limited engagement with patients. Physical therapy allows you to be with people who are taking responsibility for their health." Dorsett felt that she was finally doing what she was supposed to be doing. "In becoming a physical therapist, I felt like I arrived at the right work," she says.

There were other relationships. During the three years she worked with Vision Quest, Dorsett had become involved with

Dan Hostetler, who worked with the kids part-time as a carpenter and wheelwright on the wagon trains. She and Dan, who was 10 years her junior, corresponded when she went back to school, seeing each other when they could.

After earning a physical therapy degree at Hahnemann Medical College and working for a time at a neurodevelopment institute at Rutgers University in New Jersey, Dorsett discovered she was pregnant. Three years after she left Vision Quest, she and Dan decided to marry and, in an act of generosity on both sides, Dorsett and her family, with whom she was now reconciled, planned a traditional Baltimore wedding. Now 43 and three months pregnant, she walked down a garden path to a trellised arch in her mother's back yard, dressed in a lovely white dress, carrying a beautiful bouquet of pink flowers arranged by Mrs. Edmunds and her garden club, to meet Dan and an officiant at the bottom of the sloping yard. She was accompanied by both parents, now divorced, each of whom took an arm, accompanying her with almost comic determination to lead their daughter to domesticity. Dorsett radiated love and good will as she did in all other parts of her life, and the wedding party that followed was an elegant affair with contemporary music (Dan was a musician), catered with canapés presented on apricot table-cloths under a white tent.

Two weeks after their wedding, Dorsett and Dan moved to Tucson, Arizona, Dan's home. After all her brave adventures, Dorsett found this move very difficult, a profound uprooting from all she had known. Dan continued to work with Vision Quest, sometimes traveling for months with the covered wagons while Dorsett stayed in Tucson with their baby, Gabriel, and a new life. She found work as a physical therapist at the University of Arizona Medical Center, but while she was nursing Gabe, she worked in the mornings and stayed home with Gabe in the afternoons, learning how to be happy alone at home with a baby. Dan's mother took the baby while Dorsett was working.

Daycare would continue to be a stitched-together challenge. For two years, Dorsett found a woman who kept Gabe and three other children in her home, and then, when Gabe was in nursery, pre-kindergarten and elementary school, Dorsett would work during the school hours, sometimes leaving Gabe in after-school programs.

Dan left the marriage when Gabe was four years old, and they divided their time with him after that. "The hardest part of my life occurred when my marriage failed," Dorsett says. "The divisiveness, the pain...the divorce was really hard but really necessary. It just wasn't working."

She adds, "My greatest joy was having a child. I had to learn how to be happy as a full- time mother with Gabe when he was an infant and I was mostly without Dan to share the joy of having a baby. But there was so much of it I loved. Nursing him until he was two-and-a-half, finding a good school for him, teaching him to ride a bike, going to his soccer games, helping him find a college ..."

Dorsett continued to work as a physical therapist at the University of Arizona Medical Center, and in private practice, through Gabe's childhood and college years. At the same time, she became more and more involved with the sanctuary movement in Tucson, volunteering her therapy services at a local refugee clinic. Her interest in alternative healing led her to zero balancing, a mind/body technique using human anatomical structure to release energy that will relieve chronic pain, among other results. During her training, she met John Hamwee, a British practitioner living in the English hill country, whose book *Zero Balancing: Touching the Energy of Bone* is dedicated to her. Dorsett and John have had a long-distance relationship for the last 30 years, communicating often, meditating together via Skype, and meeting when they can, in spite of their geographical separation.

Needing to pay for Gabe's college tuition and her own mortgage, Dorsett worked at the Medical Center until she was almost 70, when she felt that she had learned all she could from the job. Her colleagues at work were beginning to consider her "too old," taking too much billable time with clients in a more fast-paced medical environment, and suggested that it was time for her to retire. With bills still to pay and an unquenchable curiosity, Dorsett turned to one more dream that she had been carrying around for a few decades: she wanted to learn more about acupuncture as a healing technique. She cut back on work to take one course, then another, until she realized that she loved the work, and the challenge of learning something new excited her. Finally enrolling full-time in acupuncture school, Dorsett found herself a year later, at 71, the spokesperson at her graduation. "We hadn't picked a speaker," Dorsett says, "and I felt I had something to say and spontaneously went up to the podium and spoke extemporaneously to the class." Using the liberation and privilege that comes with age, Dorsett delivered an inspirational speech to classmates. Her extra decades of wisdom, not to mention her sustained energy and engagement, has to have set a powerful example of a life fully lived.

Dorsett looked inside herself to find her mission to make the world better in service to her community. Sylvia Drew Ivie, civil rights lawyer and health care advocate, breathed it in from the environment in which she was raised.

The Civil Rights Lawyer: Sylvia's Story

Sylvia Drew Ivie learned early that she was expected to do something with her life that would contribute to the improvement of her world. That was a non-negotiable expectation from her mother, Minnie Drew. So, Sylvia, a pretty Black girl with large, expressive eyes, and long black hair down her back, may have had a clearer idea than some of us that she would do more than work for a couple of years, marry, and have children. Throughout her career, as a young lawyer at the NAACP Legal Defense Fund, litigating significant civil rights cases, as executive director of the National Health Law Program (NHelp) and later a community health clinic, testifying on behalf of health access before state and U.S. legislative bodies, she has never lost her sense of purpose.

If we were to assemble a step-by-step chronological understanding of Sylvia's life's work through the influence of people and circumstances, the first stepping stone would be her mother, with her embrace of a Quaker philosophy of service. The second step would be a pivotal community service weekend in East Harlem, while she was a student at Oakwood, a Quaker boarding school in Poughkeepsie, New York. The third would be her experience as a member of the Class of '65 at Vassar, in that it taught her to seek an environment in which she did not feel so isolated from the Black community. This insight led to the fourth step – the decision to go to law school at Howard University instead of Harvard. The fifth, and perhaps most significant, was the influence of Dr. Montague Cobb, a noted anthropologist and physician, who taught her about the structure of separatism, particularly as it applies to health care. These are the stories Sylvia tells when she talks about her life.

Sylvia's place in the demographic of the class, as one of two African American students, would have a profound effect on some of her crucial life decisions. I knew of Sylvia – we all knew the names of the two Black students in the class – but I had never met her at Vassar. She came to college having grown up among the African American elite centered around the community of Howard University, the historically Black institution of higher education in Washington, DC. Her background, interesting on its own and as an integral part of her identity and self-confidence, provides both a profound counterpoint to her experience at Vassar and a context for the influences that have enabled her to fulfill her mother's expectations. We begin with her family.

Sylvia's father, Dr. Charles Drew, earned national renown for his work with blood banks during World War II. "My father did not invent blood banks, as is sometimes reported," Sylvia says. "His work was not seminal. His contribution, which he developed with a Canadian colleague, was to devise and patent a filter, using potassium, that kept blood plasma from spoiling when banked." Dr. Drew first worked on the problem of banking blood to provide plasma to burned patients after a hospital fire in Montreal, saving many lives.

Continuing his work at Columbia University, while working with a team setting up blood banks, Dr. Drew applied his filter so that plasma would survive transport overseas. "His potassium filter did the trick," Sylvia says, "turning the plasma into a quality product." Sylvia, who is often asked to speak about her father's career, notes that he next worked at Johns Hopkins University, where he encountered a U.S. Navy directive that plasma for blood banks could not be collected from African Americans. After strongly objecting to this policy, on the ground that the quality of blood has nothing to do with skin color, he succeeded in getting the Navy to accept blood from Black donors, but agreed to label the blood by race. This was enough of an affront to him, however, that he soon moved his teaching and research to Freedmen's Hospital, in Washington, DC, the first hospital established in the nineteenth century to treat former enslaved people, now a teaching hospital at Howard University. It was there that Charles and his wife Minnie settled their family – three daughters and a son – in a house on the Howard campus.

Sylvia, their third child, was six years old when her father, then 45, was killed in an automobile accident. Though Charles

Drew was the famous parent, it was Minnie who set the children on their life courses.

Minnie navigated the largely segregated Washington, DC public-school system on behalf of her children. Sylvia's two older sisters were students at the academic Roosevelt High School in DC – sister Bebe (named BB for "blood bank" by the maternity nurses attending her birth) began her high school education at Roosevelt, but transferred to Dunbar High School. Sister Charlene, who would later become a prominent Washington political figure, finished, but not happily, at Roosevelt. After the experience of the other girls, Minnie was reluctant to put Sylvia into the Washington public high school system and, looking for another option, turned to the Quakers for Sylvia's high school education. The Quaker connection is not accidental. Though Sylvia and her family have never confirmed the whole story, they believe that Minnie's grand-mother had been rescued by the Quakers from slavery in North Carolina and brought through their network to Phila-delphia, where Minnie grew up, immersed in the Quaker community there. In Washington, the Drew family belonged to a Unitarian church that had a successfully integrated com-munity.

Minnie sent Sylvia to the Quaker boarding school, Oak-wood. "My mother put me on a train all by myself, at 13, to go to Poughkeepsie, and from the moment I arrived at Oakwood, I felt welcome and comfortable there," Sylvia remembers. She thrived academically, acted in plays, joined the Shakespeare Club and participated in student government. She particularly remembers a significant community service experience arranged through the American Friends Service Committee – a weekend trip to East Harlem in New York to paint apartments of older people. "To be sure I could go, I faked my mom's signature on a permission slip, and went to New York, where I was housed with a Puerto Rican family. I was so moved," Sylvia says, "when my host, a young boy, took me to his home and I saw that this large family had emptied a whole room in their small apartment in order to give me a private accommodation. Such generosity! I learned so much that weekend." Sylvia remembers that experience as pivotal to her commitment to public service.

Proximity to Vassar while she was at Oakwood, right there in Poughkeepsie, certainly had an influence on Sylvia's decision to put the college on her list – that and the fact that she was offered a generous scholarship there, and that Radcliffe, her other choice, had waitlisted her. Her difficult experience at the college, documented earlier, in that cultural stew of racism in which we all lived, some of us without much awareness, did not keep Sylvia from succeeding as a student or participating as a citizen in the important work of the civil rights movement during her college years.

The same summer, after her sophomore year at Vassar, when Sylvia went to Mississippi to help sign up school children to attend white schools, she also walked through another door that opened up her world. She was recruited to help in the office of one of her father's illustrious colleagues from Amherst and Howard – anthropologist and physician William Montague Cobb. After earning his medical degree at Howard University, Dr. Cobb stayed to teach there, focusing his interest on racial biology. One event that sparked his interest in the subject was the controversy over American athlete Jesse Owens' extraordinary performance in the 1936 Olympics in Berlin. Owens' four gold medals incensed Adolf Hitler, who claimed that Black people had larger bones, giving them an unfair advantage in track and field events. Cobb's further study would put a lie to Hitler's claim, and he went on to be the first African American to earn a Ph.D. in biocultural anthropology, with a focus on the idea of race and its negative impact on communities of color.

At the time Sylvia began doing summer work with him, Dr. Cobb was president of the National Medical Association, and editor of its *Journal*. Because he was an important spokesman for health care equity, he was invited to be part of the leadership team organizing the participation of Black physicians in the paradigm shifting 1963 March on Washington, at which Dr. Martin Luther King, Jr. made his famous "I have a dream" speech. This provided Sylvia's second opportunity that summer to be in the same room with a civil rights icon. Dr. Cobb took her to an organizing meeting, in which she sat, as quietly and unobtrusively as possible, looking into the "magnetic eyes" of Dr. King. At the march itself, Sylvia recalls, "With 300,000 people on the Mall, I sat in the third row, swallowed up by the most peaceful, beatific spirit. There was a sense that we were sharing a collective problem, and I felt such good will as we held hands with crossed arms and sang 'We shall overcome!'"

During college summers, Sylvia helped Dr. Cobb produce the *NMA Journal*, and in the process learned from his profiles of Black physicians, and from his editorials, the status of medical care and medical insurance in the Black community. Dr. Cobb was a careful teacher and, with two daughters of his own, he took an interest in showing Sylvia the structure of separatism in health care. She already knew about separate housing and separate schools – what Dr. Cobb demonstrated for her was a deeply rooted and institutionally supported health care divide between Black and White patients.

The National Medical Association (NMA) was, for example, the organization for African American physicians who were unable to join the American Medical Association (AMA). As Sylvia learned from Dr. Cobb, to become a member of the AMA, a doctor was first required to be professionally recognized locally. Black doctors did not have admitting privileges in most mainstream hospitals, and hospitals took patients through doctors with admitting privileges. Thus most hospitals did not admit Black patients. And because Black doctors did not have hospital privileges, they were not eligible for the AMA, an important organization through which doctors built collegial relationships and learned about medical innovations. The NMA would provide that for African American physicians.

Among the illustrious African American thinkers who had been colleagues of her father, Dr. Cobb would be the most important mentor to Sylvia in constructing her career. She did not know then what kind of work she would do; she knew only that in her family, it was a given that she would complete college and graduate school. She might, like Dr. Cobb, pursue anthropology, or perhaps social work, but as she thought about it, the practice of law began to emerge as "the right tool for the moment." After being accepted at both Harvard Law School and Howard University Law School, she debated her choice while at home for spring vacation. To help her make a decision, her mother brought in another heavy hitter in the Black community, another Amherst friend of her father: Judge William Hastie, appointed by Harry Truman in 1949 to be a judge on the Third Circuit of the U.S. Court of Appeals. He was another fierce civil rights advocate in Sylvia's orbit, a Harvard Law School graduate who argued strongly for Sylvia to choose Harvard. But after her experience at Vassar, she wasn't eager to put herself in another elite, largely white environment, especially when she also would have been one of only a few women there. "When Judge Hastie came to talk to me, I think he and my mother were underwhelmed by my gratitude. Finally, he gave up, saying as he got up to leave, 'Young lady, if you don't have fire in your belly, then Harvard is not for you.'"

Sylvia was not ungrateful for Judge Hastie's interest. "I appreciated his attention. I knew I was so privileged to know all these great characters who had known my father," she says. "But Judge Hastie was wrong. I did have fire in my belly."

It was Howard law professors who were the authors of, for example, the Brown vs. the Board of Education case, argued before the Supreme Court in 1954, in which the justices ruled unanimously that racial segregation of children in public schools was unconstitutional.

Her Howard law degree led Sylvia to a first job at *the* law firm for civil rights, the NAACP Legal Defense and Education Fund, at their offices in New York City. An April 1969 cover story in *Jet Magazine* identifies Sylvia as a "rural poverty specialist," who was instrumental in the Fund's efforts to create similar legal defense agencies for native American and Mexican American communities. The article includes photos of a beautiful Sylvia at work, the camera catching her warm, natural smile, her long dark hair pulled over one shoulder. The writer called her a "key figure" in litigation which was then being prepared against the Farmers Home Administration's practice of granting long-term loans to white farmers, and short-term loans to Black farmers. The article, written in a sexist age, made as much of her looks as her talent as a lawyer, quoting one co-worker saying, "Man, she's good. She's just too shy. I really don't think the child knows she's pretty."

Right away, Sylvia was also involved in cases of health equity. Doctors in the 1960s still had "colored" and white waiting rooms, and hospitals were still segregated. Pointing out that since Truman, the Senate and House had been fighting passage of any kind of national health insurance, especially for racial reasons, Sylvia notes that the passage of the Medicare bill into law in the summer of 1965 meant that hospitals taking Medicare were required by law to take patients regardless of color. She worked on cases in which, in violation of the law, pregnant Black women in labor had been turned away from hospitals federally funded for Medicaid patients, a large percentage of whom were Black. Sylvia's work would eventually help to break down the color barrier in hospital care.

While she was working in the New York office, Sylvia often grabbed lunch at Wolfie's Deli in Columbus Circle, a favorite lunch spot for her colleagues and journalists from the Public Broadcasting System (PBS), whose office was in the neighborhood. It was there that she met her husband, PBS journalist Ardie Ivie. When asked if she, like many of us in the Class of '65, was concerned about finding a husband in those years, she says, "No. I dated a lot, but my main focus was on work and service. That was my mother's message." She adds, "My older sister Bebe had married early and provided my mother with some grandchildren, and my sister Charlene was, like me, earning advanced degrees, she in neuroscience. Later she served the community as a council member for the District of Columbia for more than 20 years." Charlene Drew Jarvis would later become president of Southeastern University in Washington, DC, until its closure in 2009.

After they married, Sylvia and Ardie decided to move back to Washington, DC, to put themselves back in the charged environment she had known in the Howard community, and to do work that would contribute to positive social change. While Ardie could work in the Washington office of PBS, Sylvia wanted to try a new project. She was given an opportunity that would set in motion a career she continues to pursue to this day, following the seeds that were planted when she had summer jobs in Dr. Cobb's office. She was asked to be the executive director of the National Health and Environmental Law Program (NHelp), a legal services organization dedicated to helping lawyers and policy makers advance access to health care, especially for Black and Brown communities. The organization works with a cadre of health and environmental experts to support the work of neighborhood lawyers serving poor and underserved populations around the country. It was the perfect job for Sylvia, one that gave her early leadership responsibilities in exactly the area of law where her heart resided. "I am a sort of timid person, and I don't like confrontation, but I needed to take a breath and push myself a little," Sylvia says. "I think having the courage to try something that is a little beyond what you already know helps you to feel more profoundly yourself."

In 1974, Ardie Ivie was one of the first people of color to be offered a fellowship by the American Film Institute to spend two years in Los Angeles writing screen plays. It was a dream of his that Sylvia supported, so the couple moved to the west coast, where she could continue her work with NHelp. Ardie wrote a screen play called *Mustache*, about his father, who had been a train conductor, that earned praise from critics. But at the conclusion of that fellowship, a career in screenwriting did not materialize.

By that time there were two children in the family – a daughter, Leslie, and a son, Drew – and they decided to stay on the west coast. As his career developed as a writer and a print and TV journalist, Ardie had the luxury of being able to work at home, so he and Sylvia essentially switched traditional roles: she went out to work, and Ardie managed the household, cooked dinner, and supervised Leslie and Drew. Because he had never finished earning a bachelor's degree, Sylvia encouraged him to go back to college. He attended classes at the University of California at Los Angeles (UCLA), where he eventually earned a doctoral degree in education. In addition to writing articles and reviews as a freelance writer, Ardie worked in the office of the Vice Chancellor of Student Affairs and the Office of the President, producing summer programs for historically Black colleges.

There was another health connection for Sylvia in Los Angeles, though one that she would not involve herself with until much later in her career. In August 1965, the Watts neighborhood of Los Angeles would become the first to erupt in race riots that would convulse many of America's cities in the late 1960s. In the following months, California governor Edmund Brown assembled an eight-member commission to examine the causes of the Watts Rebellion, and to suggest remedies. The McCone Commission, as it was called, cited poor health status and diminished access to healthcare in the Watts neighborhood as major factors contributing the upheaval in Watts in the summer of 1965. One response was the establishment of the Charles R. Drew University of Medicine and Science, incorporated in 1966 to train medical professionals "dedicated to social justice and health equity for underserved populations," according to the University's website. The University was named after Sylvia's father, acknowledging his prominence as a pioneering African American physician. More than 50 years later, the university, which is recognized as a Historically Black Graduate Institution, has trained more than 600 physicians and thousands of other health professionals, most of whom are Black or Latinx. Interestingly, at the beginning, 80 percent of students were Black; now the student population is 60 percent Latinx.

Sylvia, meanwhile, was gaining prominence for her own health advocacy work, so much so that near the end of President Jimmy Carter's only term, she was invited to Washington, DC to head the Office of Civil Rights under the Secretary of Health, Education and Welfare, Patricia Roberts Harris. Because Sylvia had moved west for Ardie's career, and because it was a government appointment, and they knew it would be temporary, Sylvia took a leave of absence from NHelp to take the government post. She and Ardie agreed to have a bicoastal marriage, in which the children – Leslie, at five years old, and Drew, at seven months – would remain at home in Los Angeles with Ardie and the children's caretaker, Miss Belfield, and Sylvia would commute to Washington, coming home some weekends. "Ardie wasn't happy with this idea," Sylvia says, "but I think he felt bad about uprooting me from the east coast for his fellowship, and he wanted to support this opportunity for me to take on an important government assignment." The job and the commute lasted seven months: President Carter lost the 1980 election to Ronald Reagan.

This turned out to be an exciting but ultimately frustrating seven months for Sylvia. Guidelines that would clarify specific details in the administration of Title VII, the civil rights laws passed during the Johnson Administration in 1964, had never been written. The consequence was that, more than a decade after it was enacted, the law was very difficult to apply. "For example," Sylvia explains, "the law stipulated that any entity that gets federal funding cannot discriminate on the basis of race or ethnicity. Under an earlier legislation, the Hill-Burton Act, a number of new hospitals had been built in the south, using federal dollars. The Act, the Hospital Survey and Construction Act of 1946, was enacted to improve the quality and supply of hospital beds throughout the U.S., but in the messy process of legislation, it also codified 'separate but equal' access to hospitals. Those hospitals were still refusing to admit people of color, particularly Black women in labor."

It was Sylvia's assignment to draft the guidelines that would put teeth into Title VII, some of which covered exactly the issue on which she had focused her career – equal access to health care. She was anxious to accomplish this task, but, sadly, she did not have the support of the Secretary of HEW, who, Sylvia felt, did not approve of her progressive politics. During her time in the federal government, she found ways of getting around the hospital discrimination issues, however. When she was called to clarify the details of the Act with regard to health care, in the absence of guidelines she drafted that were never approved, Sylvia would write a letter outlining her interpretation of the policy. That letter would serve in place of guidelines. Actual guidelines were not approved until 1994, 20 years later. The experience was a disappointing introduction to the sometimes glacial pace of government action. "I learned to work around the roadblocks," she says, "but it was a missed opportunity."

When Sylvia went back to Los Angeles, her family, and NHelp at the end of Carter's presidency, in January 1981, she had more battles with government ahead of her, and more opportunities to lend her voice to change. The Reagan Administration's Justice Department, under the leadership of Attorney General Ed Meese, had mounted a campaign to cut funds to legal services organizations like NHelp that encouraged neighborhood activism. In an effort to "kill the generals" – the legal advisors to local and neighborhood organizations – Meese sought to reduce the number of class action suits against the government that these legal experts were organizing for underserved populations. As part of their campaign, lawyers from the Department of Justice would make unscheduled visits to the NHelp offices, examining files, harassing the organization and interrupting its work. "We were waging war against Neanderthals," Sylvia said. "After 10 years, it was time for me to move on and for the organization to have new leadership."

Sharpening her focus on community health care, she became executive director of the THE (To Help Everyone) Clinic in South Los Angeles. What appealed to Sylvia about the clinic was that it was, first, nonpolitical, and second, an agency that provided direct health care services to underserved populations. The organization was started by eight white women, mostly nurses, whose focus was on what women could do for women. It began as a women's health center, but began treating men as well when it started to receive government funds designated for community clinics that would not allow the clinic to discriminate on the basis of gender. As director of the clinic, Sylvia was able to collect rich personal stories about the population THE serves, stories that she could carry to the California State Legislature in Sacramento and the U.S. Congress, when she, as head of a health care organization, was invited to testify on health care. The clinic gave Sylvia a platform to affect policies that would benefit the health care of the populations she had dedicated her career to serve. When she left THE, after 16 years, the clinic had eight branches in South Los Angeles, and it remains a thriving organization. Sylvia left to be with Ardie when he was diagnosed with brain cancer in 2003. He died at 59 in 2005.

As a widow, Sylvia found more opportunities to support access to health care, with work that continues to occupy her in her 70s. In the early 2000s, five Los Angeles city hospitals were under scrutiny for their financial health and the quality of care they were providing. One of those, the least financially stressed, was Martin Luther King Hospital, the teaching hospital for Charles Drew University. After news of poor-quality care in two of the hospital's medical cases made its way to the *Los Angeles Times*, the city closed King for several years, leaving South Los Angeles without one of its hospitals and Drew University without a training facility. Sylvia was asked to join a steering committee on the future of Drew King Medical Center. In doing so, she became a member of the Drew team, where she is now Special Assistant for Community Affairs, working for the president of Drew.

Looking back, Sylvia acknowledges that her father's name and reputation have opened doors for her. "I think it was my exposure to Dr. Cobb that led me to invest in civil rights as a cause," she continues, "but I was not ambitious, not driven. I wanted to be a willing helper. I have a deep curiosity and affection for people. That's my gift. I care about people. I look for opportunities to connect and be helpful."

As young women, both Dorsett and Sylvia had big ideas

and big ambitions to make the world a better place. As their lives unfolded, both women narrowed the scope of their ambitions to focus on tangible change that they could make with their own efforts. Both women are still, in their late 70s, working toward those tangible changes.

CHAPTER 6

Reinventing Motherhood

"Discovering La Leche League influenced me ... to dedicate my-self to mothering ..."

Ros Anderson Nesticò

We were also rethinking motherhood. I had my first baby in 1970. For the purposes of timeline in this book, I will label the decade of the 1970s as the childbearing years for the Vassar Class of '65. In this new phase of our lives, we were still operating in the midst of the ferment and the revolutions that were taking place around us. We were inventing all kinds of new rules, including new rules for parenting. It was hard, but also exhilarating, to know that, as with everything else, we were making it up as we went along.

For many in our age cohort, having a baby was a political and feminist act. Members of the Class of '65 became mothers during a renaissance of old ideas about childbirth, including a belief in the benefits to infants of natural childbirth – giving birth without the help of anesthetics. Then there was breast-feeding, supported by the La Leche League, a program founded by seven nursing mothers from suburban Chicago in 1956. It was the La Leche League, along with the return to natural practices that encouraged young mothers to reconsider breastfeeding their babies.

We were inspired then, though we didn't know it, by anthropologist Margaret Mead, who came of age just as women earned the right to vote. It was she who, among other contributions to the women's movement, encouraged modern educated American women to practice natural childbirth, embracing motherhood as "a conscious human purpose and not a burden imposed by the flesh." The term "natural childbirth" was coined by Grantly Dick-Read, a physician whose book *Childhood Without Fear* was published in 1942, and became a classic. In *The Feminine Mystique,* Betty Friedan notes that the natural childbirth movement Mead inspired "was not at all a return to primitive earth-mother maternity. It appealed to the independent, educated, spirited American woman ... because it enabled her to experience childbirth not as a mindless female animal ... but as a whole person, able to control her own body with her aware mind."

Most of the mothers I have interviewed for this book had their babies using a natural childbirth technique called the "Lamaze Method." The method included childbirth education classes, training in relaxation and breathing techniques, and the involvement of the father. The method was introduced in France in 1951 by Dr. Fernand Lamaze, who had observed similar techniques in Russia. By the late 1950s, the Lamaze Method had been introduced in the U.S., and by 1960, a nonprofit organization supporting the Lamaze Method had been founded. Perhaps the idea also found fertile ground in the women's movement. It provided an opportunity to challenge the existing orthodoxy of the male obstetrical establishment, and its practice of anesthetizing the mother, the star of the show in her biggest role – and her unborn baby – with spinal or caudal anesthesia. Obstetricians, understandably, were interested in getting the baby out with a minimum of fuss from her or, God forbid, a father in the delivery room.

My husband John and I had our own experience with natural childbirth. I was pregnant with my daughter Katrina when John and I moved to Vermont in 1970. It was important to me that I participate consciously in the birth of my baby, doing the physical work myself. That first summer in Stowe, Vermont, I found an obstetrician in nearby Barre who reluctantly agreed to allow me to deliver my baby without the intervention of drugs that would put poison in the baby's bloodstream, and with John present in the delivery room. John and I signed up for Lamaze childbirth classes in Burlington, Vermont's biggest city, an hour away.

In Lamaze classes, we learned to think of childbirth as an experience shared by husband and wife, in which the husband would act as a coach throughout the training and labor process and as a witness who would be present for the arrival of his offspring, and cheer his wife on in the delivery room.

Relenting after much negotiation, my doctor said, sternly, "I will withhold anesthesia and allow John to be in the delivery room, IF you understand that I will ask him to leave, and administer the needle if the medical situation calls for it." Armed with my training, I was pretty smug about my ability to power through childbirth, and John, always a practical, do-it-yourself person, performed well. By the time my daughter Erika was born, four years later with the same aspirations, my doctor was inured to Lamaze techniques. "Your husband will want to be with you, I assume," he said. "But the same rules apply..."

I was thrilled to be pregnant with both babies. I felt physically strong and healthy and something akin to athletic for the first time in my life. The experience of delivering Katrina left me feeling powerful and tough. There was something triumphant about being a woman in the experience of childbirth – a triumph I felt probably for the first time in my life. Perhaps I had never considered myself physically powerful or even capable – I, who held the position of seventh team center on the Springside School hockey team, was a bench warmer in basketball practice, swinging my legs on the sidelines in my blue tunic and bloomers, who after years of ski lessons still cowered at the sight of a mogul.

The earthiness of that era, the self-sufficiency of it all, was in a physical and practical way both feminine and feminist. Self-sufficiency in women's health was a central thesis of a popular book, *Our Bodies Ourselves*, published by the Boston Women's Health Collective in 1973. Researched and written by women, the book covered all aspects of women's health, from sexuality and gender identification to birth control, pregnancy, childbirth and menopause. The book was written from the perspective of women's own experience, and embraced the idea that women should take independent responsibility for understanding the functions of their own bodies. It captured and encouraged the personal power we were beginning to feel.

The renaissance of breastfeeding was another return to the authentic, healthy order of life, another orthodoxy to embrace. This is where classmate Rosalind Nesticò's story comes in.

The Breastfeeding Advocate: Rosalind's Story

Rosalind Anderson Nesticò didn't find her mission to promote the benefits of breastfeeding – or her vocation as a pioneering lactation consultant in Italy – until she was a mother herself, struggling to define her life in a new country. In taking up that mission, Ros, an American, would become a leader in Italy of one of the significant movements of our generation. Like other pioneers in the Class of '65, Ros, too, became a midwife to the revolutions that marked our era.

Ros' interest in La Leche League had bloomed with the birth of her first child, Filippo, whom she had wanted to breastfeed. She did not realize that aspiration with Filippo, however: neither mother nor son were given the time or support to figure out how to do it. That was disappointing to her. Before the birth of her second child, her daughter Florinda, two years later, Ros came across the La Leche League's book *The Womanly Art of Breastfeeding*. The book had been written by two of the Chicago women who had started La Leche in 1956, to share the wisdom of women experienced in breastfeeding. This discovery changed the course of Ros' life.

Though breastfeeding was more common in Italy, like the rest of our age cohort, Ros was up against a long history of attitudes about the practice, its practicality, aesthetics and value. Alternatives to breastfeeding, principally wet nurses, women who breastfed other women's babies, have been available since the beginning of recorded history. Scientifically produced baby formula has been sold since the 19th century. But over the centuries, through times when breastfeeding has gone in and out of fashion, especially for middle-class women, breast milk has been thought to be the perfect food for babies, both comforting to the baby and offering a rich natural diet that was sufficient to his nutritional needs. In post-World War II America, the era of our childhood, baby formula had been embraced by the medical establishment as the feeding regimen of choice, and in our childhood, only 20 percent of American women breastfed their babies.

There was a physicality to the experience that put some women off. For my own mother, for example, breastfeeding represented too intimate a contact for her sensibilities. In the

1950s, newspapers were not even permitted to use the word "breastfeeding," an unacceptable reference to a part of a woman's body, in print. "Nursing," on the other hand, was okay. Hospitals and doctors encouraged the use of formula for its convenience. The La Leche book, which sold 17,000 copies in its first five years, has been updated a number of times in the more than 60 years that La Leche League has been in existence.

Looking back, Ros now says of breastfeeding Filippo, "Essentially it was sabotaged by the experience in the clinic with the nuns and the whole business of test-weighing babies," all, she points out, "in the delicate phase when the new mother is trying to bring her milk in abundantly." Disappointed and guilty about her inability to breastfeed her son, she felt that she had not, in her own mind, proven her worth as a mother. Her regret about that affected her relationship with Filippo as he was growing up. "I wish I'd been able to let it go," she reflects now, "but especially when breastfeeding became my main interest, my 'failure' with him loomed large in my mind and he was aware of my guilt." Would she have felt that way 10 years earlier? Probably not. We were all in the grip of new standards by which we judged ourselves.

"Our relationship was also affected by my feeling out of place at home, and not doing a good job of the whole business," she adds. She had, until her son's birth, been out of the house, working. Though she might have left her children with her mother-in-law, Ros couldn't see the point of going back to work as an American woman in Italy where her only employment opportunities might have been to teach English or be an English-speaking store clerk. In that way, she had chosen an environment for raising her children that was in contrast to the environment in which she was raised.

Ros grew up in Tallahassee, Florida, the state capital, in a grand house built in 1929 by her grandfather, a manufacturer of bricks used in building Florida's roads, just as the American stock market crashed and the Great Depression began. Ros' father, a newspaper man, and her mother, who wrote for the Florida State University (FSU) news bureau, had four children, spaced over 23 years. Ros was the second child, born nine years after her older sister, two years before her younger sister and 14 years before a baby brother came along. Because their mother worked, the children would come home to their grandmother, who lived with them. Ros grew up with a mother who, though she didn't call herself a feminist, provided a model for a woman involved in the world outside the home. Ros always considered herself a feminist, without defining for herself exactly what that meant.

Ros worked hard at Vassar, always feeling under pressure to prove herself equal to the college's standards. She had had a traumatic experience in freshman English, "after the first hour test, when the instructor called me in and said this wouldn't do if I wanted to be an English major," she remembers. She went on to major in English, but because of that early experience, and though she was on the dean's list, she never really felt confident as a "Vassar girl."

After college, she says, "I didn't want to get serious yet. I wanted to go to Europe – I had taken Italian and become interested in art history, and the vocational office had given me the name of a school in Florence where I could study Italian." She convinced her mother to go with her on a two-month tour of Europe, ending in Italy, in the fall of 1965. At the end of the trip, her mother went home and Ros stayed in Florence, finding housing in a *pensione* and studying Italian.

She met her future husband, Aldo Nesticò, who was studying law, almost right away. On a trip home the following summer, Ros found herself pining to get back to Italy. "I love the Italian language (I love language in general – I think I got that from my father who loved to read the dictionary), and it was fun and exciting to get to know a whole different people ... with a companion, my husband Aldo, an Italian himself, and an excellent teacher." Ros points out that Italians are quite forgiving of speakers butchering their language – they appreciate the effort. And their passion for food and eating was one that she came to embrace. "I've made it my own." Perhaps most importantly, in Italy, "family is a fundamental and strong force," Ros says. Ros' own understanding of a strong attachment to family began with her grandfather's idea to create a grand, family-centered enclave in Tallahassee, one that her father, whose own home and family life were interrupted, perpetuated in his will. Ros and her siblings are still able to go home to that big house in Tallahassee every year.

Ros and Aldo were married in Italy in the fall of 1966. In the five years between their marriage and the birth of their son Filippo, she worked as a secretary to the director of the Florida State University Study Center in Florence, improving her Italian, getting a good salary. When Filippo was born, Ros left her job. "I didn't initially decide not to work outside the home after having children," she says. "It just worked out that way. And discovering La Leche League influenced me, of course, to dedicate myself to mothering." It turned out that being a homemaker – keeping house, cooking, taking care of children – was a big job. But she didn't feel "creative," as her parents were in their lives. Through motherhood, though, she would find her own creativity.

Ros couldn't redo her breastfeeding experience for Filippo, but through La Leche she came to understand what had gone wrong the first time – that her confidence in her own ability to produce milk had been undermined by the nuns' concerns about the timing of feedings and the baby's weight. She was determined to successfully breastfeed her next baby. Meanwhile, she volunteered to gather a group of breastfeeding women in her house for monthly support meetings on the La Leche model. She provided the group emotional and practical support, derived from other women's experience with breast-feeding. Breastfeeding was a more common practice in Italy, and soon Ros was involved with a La Leche group both in Florence and in Milan. When Florinda was born, Ros had been involved with the League for three years. She used what she had learned to nurse the baby successfully for several years. Ros would soon become a leader in the program, and by 1979, three years after the birth of Florinda, La Leche Italia had been established, in large part due to her contributions.

In 1985, La Leche League donated 40 thousand dollars to help create the International Board of Lactation Consultant Examiners (IBLCE), which established and certified lactation standards, breastfeeding support from a growing group of health volunteers – lactation consultants. Because more and more new mothers were choosing to breastfeed their babies, there was a growing demand for support for those women. For almost 20 years, Ros worked as a leader and lay consultant, helping nursing mothers, until she decided to become certified as a lactation consultant herself.

IBLCE had created an exam to prepare people who were already health professionals to be lactation consultants, but volunteers like Ros could take the exam only by first taking a series of 14 health sciences courses. Dedicated to her calling, Ros took the courses long distance, sat for the exam in Miami Beach, on a summer trip home, and became a board-certified lactation consultant in 1991. She then worked with IBLCE, consulting long distance, helping with translation, to create an exam in Italian and establish a professional level of board-certified lactation consultants in Italy. Ros would renew her certification through courses or retaking the international exam for 25 years.

But her work wasn't done. In 1991, the World Health

Organization (WHO) and the United Nations Children's Fund (UNICEF), again with support from the La Leche League, launched a new program to recognize and award hospitals that offered "an optimal level of care for infant feeding and mother/baby bonding," according to the website. These hospitals practiced "rooming in," which allowed babies to remain in their mothers' hospital rooms 24 hours per day, encouraged on-demand breastfeeding, and provided extensive encouragement and education to new mothers. "These hospitals use 'mother friendly' steps while she is in labor (companionship, water baths, walking), and non-pharmaceutical methods for pain management," Ros explains. "I embraced the Baby Friendly Initiative wholeheartedly," Ros says. "I could see its importance in improving the help women got right from the start." Once again, Ros was interested in bringing the program to Italy. In her experience, Italian hospitals were managed by nuns who believed in feeding babies on a schedule, operating on a theory borrowed from formula feeding that babies should be given bigger feeds less often. They discouraged feeding the baby any time he cried, and they did not allow the babies to stay in the room with their mothers. The baby friendly hospital program is now well established in Italy, thanks in large part to Ros' effort. Asked if the nuns have embraced the program, she says, "I don't think many nuns are still involved in maternity wards anymore. The decision to become baby friendly either comes from the ground up, from the staff, or from top-down as an administrative decision." When hospitals are awarded the designation "Baby Friendly," she says, "it means something truly important."

"I'm quite proud of what we've done in this country."

There was one more orthodoxy embraced by our generation in the 1960s and '70s, that of limiting population growth. John and I, then settled in the progressive young exurban community we found in Stowe, Vermont, were also influenced by the Zero Population Growth (ZPG) movement, surely a response to the baby boom, the population burst following World War II. It was a cause embraced by both feminists and environmental activists – feminists, perhaps thinking of the burdens on a woman of raising too many children to allow her to pursue a life of her own; environmentalists thinking, of course, of overpopulation depleting the resources of an exhausted earth. ZPG promoted the belief that, for the good of the environment, couples should commit themselves to having only two children, "replacing only themselves" in the population. I remember that as a child raised alone among adults. I dreamed of presiding over a brood of children. But by the time my husband John and I were ready to start our own family, we were committed, earnestly, to bringing only two into the world. We had our second daughter, Erika, in 1974.

I can see now that we could be tiresomely earnest. The attitudes of my generation of women toward childbirth and postnatal care also provide another contrast between us and the generations of women and men that have followed us. We saw ourselves on a moral high ground, taking very seriously our responsibilities to adhere to natural practices. We were improving on what our mothers did, and we rigidly embraced the natural childbirth techniques then in vogue.

I only began to understand my own inflexibility on the subject when I witnessed my daughters and their husbands making decisions about their babies. My older daughter had no sanctimonious ideas about forgoing anesthesia in childbirth, and was interested only in the safe delivery of her children. My younger daughter and her husband cared more about natural childbirth techniques, but were not obsessive about it. Breastfeeding, for both, was a given. Hospitals now routinely provide lactation consultants, like Ros, to coach new mothers in how to breastfeed their babies. I see now that our daughters regarded our moral attachment to natural childbirth with some eye-rolling amusement.

CHAPTER 7

Working Mothers

"There were those that married early and had their families and then went back into the work world, and those that stayed in the work world and had their families late. And the meshugganahs who tried to do it all in their twenties, which is what I always feel lucky to have survived."

From the Bank Street conversations

The central issue and one of the most difficult challenges facing the Vassar Class of '65 was learning to manage both the demands of family and the new opportunities for women in the workplace. It was a challenge for which we had no models, no preparation and little support in the court of public opinion. We were cobbling together both the resources we needed and the rationale for our choices as we went along. We were making it up.

Classmate Deborah Detchon Dodds, who grew up in Lake Forest, Illinois, remembers a revelatory moment when she was in her thirties. "Driving home from class at the end of one day, I found myself crying and crying at the wheel of my car, sitting in a traffic jam. I thought, 'What am I crying about? This is what I wanted.' And I gave myself a little lecture, sitting in the car that day. 'You can do this. You have to be able to do this.'"

Debby could have joined the Junior League, as her mother wanted her to, in an effort to meet people in Pittsburgh, Pennsylvania, her new city, but she had decided against that. Her husband, Bob, was just beginning his law practice, and their two boys were in private school. Bob wanted her to help pay school tuitions, so he suggested she go back to work. The pair had married soon after college and Debby had been a Head Start teacher in Philadelphia while Bob was in law school. She had stopped working when she had the boys. But when Bob asked for her help, she thought, "I have the time and the ability and, well, I'll be a lawyer, too. I was free." So, she applied to and was accepted at the University of Pittsburgh law school. She was pleased that she was making good use of her time, and that her life was full with family and the prospect of a career. "I thought I was on top of it all, but" she says, recalling that moment, "I didn't know how exhausted I was."

Another classmate, Mary Mapes Watson, had always planned to have a career, and marriage and children would be a part of that plan. After college and a secretarial course, Mary held a series of support jobs, until, from her observations as secretary to the president of *Fortune Magazine*, at the business end of publishing, she became interested in marketing. Her work trajectory ultimately led her to International Paper, where she was named director, then vice president, for new product development. One more high-powered job at a competing private marketing firm would cap her career.

After graduation, Mary was having a lot of fun, interested

in the subject matter of her work in marketing, learning new skills, living in her own apartment, and enjoying a New York social life. She was in no hurry to get married until, at 30, she met Gordon Watson, who worked at *Life Magazine* at the time. Gordon was appreciative and supportive of Mary's work, so that when they married, in 1973, neither of them expected that she would interrupt her career for a full-time domestic life.

By the time they had children, Mary and Gordon were living in Bronxville and commuting to work in the city. With a reliable nanny to care for the children, daughter Sybil and son Gordon Charles, Mary felt little conflict, returning eagerly to work after each birth. But as her success grew, she was required to travel more and more across the country to meet clients. That's when she began to feel conflict between work and family. "I worried constantly about the children's care," she says. "I felt guilty about the children when I was traveling, wondering if they were okay, and thinking 'what happens when I'm not there?'" Finally, she asked the children's pediatrician if, in his opinion, she should be at home with them and he said, "Your children are fine now, but when they get to be teenagers, you need to be at home. Otherwise, you will never know what is going on with them." Persuaded that he was right, Mary "retired" at age 47, leaving her career, when Sybil and Gordon Charles became adolescents. She found part-time work in marketing, commuting to a New York office daily and returning home by 2:30 p.m., in time to greet the children on their return from school.

Debbie and Jonathan Kolb, another couple struggling to manage children and work, at first, divided their time to take care of their baby, Sam. Debbie, who was pursuing an MBA degree, took courses at night when Jonathan was available. Later, they hired *au pairs,* live-in childcare, and they had the support of a neighborhood of young families. "We had no role models," Debbie says. "Our mothers were at home, and we had no guidance about how to juggle family and work, and not much social or institutional support in place."

Each of the mothers I profile in this book had to figure out how to balance work and motherhood in her own way. Debbie and Mary Ann Mason, to be profiled later in the book, would in particular become midwives to working mothers – with their academic research and writing – helping to pave the way for the next generation of mothers in the workplace, teaching them how to negotiate for the benefits they would need to manage a family while pursuing careers, providing the guidance we didn't have.

It turns out that we can credit President Kennedy for starting the conversation about women and work, during our college years. In 1961, at the urging of social justice feminists who had been pursuing women's issues in the 30 years since the passage of the 19th Amendment to the Constitution, Kennedy set up a Presidential Commission on the Status of Women, chaired by Eleanor Roosevelt until her death in 1962. "American Women," the report from the Kennedy Commission, was published just before President Kennedy was assassinated in 1963, in our junior year.

Kennedy was a politician in touch with his times, and his rhetoric (or his speech writers) hit many of the right notes. "We are at the beginning of an era when the inroads of poverty, hunger and disease will be lessened and when men and women everywhere will have it within their power to develop their potential capacities to the maximum," he said in 1960. "In every period of national emergency, women have served with distinction in widely varied capacities but thereafter have been subject to treatment as a marginal group whose skills have been inadequately utilized." He asked the

Commission, whose membership included senators and members of Congress as well as feminist activists and educators, to assess the functions of women at home, in the economy and in society. They were to evaluate the "potential contribution of outstanding women to American life," both as working women and, in their family roles, as "transmitters of the central values of the culture."

Looking at education, employment, federal policies, and more, the Commission found that despite federal legislation, women, particularly married women, were prevented from advancing at work for many reasons, from lack of childcare support to institutional resistance to women in the workplace. To remedy the barriers to women, the Commission recommended many initiatives that are now more available, including maternity leave, daycare and after-school care, tax deductions for childcare costs and more flexibility in work schedules.

The Commission recommended continuing education opportunities for women returning to the workforce. But the language of the report betrays the commissioners' discomfort over the idea that women might choose to work, or be forced to, and raise children at the same time. "It is regrettable when women with children are forced by economic necessity," the report notes, "to seek employment while their children are young. On the other hand," they add, "those who decide to work should have childcare services available." Since married women could be expected to interrupt their work lives to raise children, the report suggested that continuing education be provided to women during their homemaking years to prepare them for the decades after age 40, when they would have the option to return to the workplace. And here's the real giveaway that the Commission had held on to some traditional views of women: "She also needs to continue her education in one form or another," the report says, "in order to provide the assistance, companionship, and stimulation needed by her husband and children as they develop." A lot of the Commission's forward thinking escaped our notice during our college years, and it took a long time for some of those recommendations to be put in place.

It is in this context that I tell my own story of an "accidental career," one that grew around the responsibilities of motherhood. I was in the vanguard of a new paradigm, figuring out, with much stress and a lot of errors, how to do it all. When I look back at myself, I see a young woman who was both earnest and naïve, ambitious and overwhelmed, competent and game, eager and exhausted, finally able to embrace her responsibilities with the mastery that comes with experience.

The Writer: Selby's Story

Somewhere in my thirties, in a literary calendar dedicated to Virginia Woolf, I found a quote attributed to her that I embraced as a mantra for myself. It was "I want everything – love, children, adventure, intimacy, and work." Yes, I thought, that is *exactly* what I want. At the time I was, with my husband and two daughters, living a domestic adventure in a yellow clapboard house on the side of a mountain in Elmore, Vermont. We were heating the house with wood, growing vegetables, buying unpasteurized milk from the dairy down the road, and I was earning a tiny income writing school board reports and feature stories for two local weekly newspapers. My husband went to work for the state government in Montpelier, my daughter Katrina was enrolled in a one-room school in the village of Elmore, and my daughter Erika was at a cooperative nursery school that a group of parents, including me, had founded in nearby Stowe. John and I were in retreat from a failed enterprise, a condominium development in the ski resort at Stowe. There, we had been in the eye of a storm, working nonstop in a family business that was bleeding money, with our babies in tow, and we were exhausted. But I had by that time, from that experience, learned that, overwhelmed as I was, I loved having work in addition to a family life.

To go back to the beginning of my story, in Philadelphia, Pennsylvania, I was a little girl firmly rooted in the 1950s. At 10 years old, learning to braid my own hair, I would have thought about a future as a wife and mother, if I thought that far ahead at all. I did write a couple of books then – one about my cat Murgatroyd giving birth to a litter of kittens, complete with illustrations – so perhaps I had a prophetic moment when I thought I might be a writer.

I was the child of older parents, who had already been married 20 years and raised one child, my brother Tommy. Like my age mates, I was a war baby, meeting my father for the first time at age two, when he returned from the Pacific front of World War II in 1945. My father was a civil engineer and my mother, a rebellious girl, came into adulthood indifferent to education and with dreams of a genteel, romantic life.

The crucible of the Depression had damaged my parents' marriage and their dreams. After a few years as an engineer working on the great American rivers helping build bridges and dams, my father spent the 1930s as a street supervisor for the gas company. My mother's rebellious nature was not, as one might have thought, evidence of a strong will so much as it was a symptom of lifelong instability. The combative teenager became a fragile, alternately frightened and angry adult. Nevertheless, unlike most of her friends, suburban Philadelphia housewives, my mother, frustrated and worn down by their perennial debt, went to work as a kindergarten teacher in a friend's nursery school in order to bring in more income. It was a job for which she had no training or education, but to her surprise, she was good at it, and she earned a salary. To earn more money, she ran a summer camp for small children in our back yard. Years later, I would come to admire her enterprise and her willingness to put herself, fearful as she was, in a workplace in which she could find competence.

Because my brother was almost 17 years older than I, my own experience at home was that of an only child. That meant my play was often solitary. I never had to fight over territory or toys with a sibling, with the result that I was probably unusually sheltered from everyday combat and competition. That circumstance may also have given me a naïve sense of my own unchallenged place in the world that bolstered me when I launched myself into a turbulent world in the 1960s. And I had three adults – my parents and my brother – advocating for me.

I went to private girls' schools and there, too, I was unencumbered by competition from braver, noisier boys. A women's college seemed a natural choice to me. My mother, sadly, had been dismissed by her father as "not college material," which may have been accurate, given her poor academic performance at boarding school, but all my adults supported me.

Neither of my parents expected that I would do anything but marry after college (more to the point, my mother hoped I would find someone with resources to support me comfortably) and have children. And that is exactly what I expected of, and hoped for, in my life. I soon discovered, however, that I didn't like all the practical realities of that dream. When I was 18, the summer before I went to Vassar, a German boyfriend, with whom I was having an intense romance, suggested that, instead of going to college, I come back to Germany to attend *Haushalt Schule* (household school), to learn to be a good

German *hausfrau*. Though I was crazy about him, I was emphatically not interested in that scenario. As I was not particularly practical, my imagined life did not include finding the perfect formula for spot removal, or washing my front stoop every morning.

I went to college, planning to continue the very good education I had received in high school – English, French, required science, singing in the chorus. The courses offered in the catalogue were a feast, and, though majoring in English, I took quite a few in anthropology, religion, mythology, philosophy, and Art 105, Vassar's popular art history survey course. Despite modest academic goals and modest achievement, I graduated enriched by the institution with a classic liberal arts education, and excited by learning, for which I will always be grateful. We lived in a kind of cocoon of privilege at Vassar, but the academic environment was one with expectations that we would be women actively engaged in the world.

Like many of my classmates, I had spent my first summer after graduation from college at a secretarial school where, after earning an expensive college degree, I learned the real stuff of the workplace for women – speed typing and shorthand. I had two early jobs in stimulating environments. The first was in New York City where I worked for the International Student Service, meeting foreign students at their ports of entry. I greeted students arriving on large passenger ships from transatlantic voyages, or at Kennedy Airport. After that adventurous year in New York City, I went on to use those secretarial skills in my second job in the office at the Theatre of the Living Arts (TLA) in Philadelphia. I spent four years, sharpening pencils, bringing coffee, and twiddling my thumbs for an elderly fundraiser, then graduating to preparing contracts and correspondence for the managing director. TLA was one of 25 regional professional theatres around the country, then very much at the forefront of theatre in the 1960s.

I had fun in both jobs, but I was not yet married, and the fear of being an old maid filled me with an acute undercurrent of anxiety during those three and a half years between college and my wedding. The prospect of a prolonged independent life was absolutely terrifying. The fact that my parents and my brother seemed equally alarmed that I had not found a husband didn't help. I had an appetite for adventure but absolutely no ability to break myself free of the idea that my life would be meaningless without a husband.

In 1968, John Holmberg and I met and married, after a quick courtship and much to everyone's relief. Though we hardly knew each other, I think we recognized familiar backgrounds and maybe a common anxiety about our ability to fit smoothly into the structure that social Philadelphia offered us. At a dinner before our wedding, my brother raised his glass for the family with a brief toast: "Thank God for John."

Shortly after we were married, we moved to the Philadelphia suburbs, from which I commuted to work every morning on the Pennsylvania Railroad with all the men, trading sections of the *Philadelphia Inquirer* as I sat next to John, and the Philadelphia Main Line rolled by outside the window. I felt no small amount of pride in that. My mother-in-law, who took a loving interest in me, invited me to join her for classes on oriental rugs and antique furniture. She used her considerable social cachet to find me a place on the women's committee of the Philadelphia Orchestra, a volunteer position that would have given me a significant boost as a suburban matron in Philadelphia. It was a coup for which I had absolutely no appreciation, I am ashamed to say. Unlike the other women, I would dash over to the meetings during my lunch hour, while they discussed fundraising schemes for the orchestra and worked on their needlepoint. I felt very superior because I got on a commuter train in the morning and I *worked*.

It turned out I wanted both the security that marriage, in

theory, gave me, and the independent work that defined me. We had been married for only a year or so when we opted for adventure and left the relative safety of Philadelphia to move to Stowe, Vermont, and run a ski lodge. John had hoped to move to Wyoming someday, where he had spent happy summers on a dude ranch, but we settled on what for me, after years of ski vacations with my brother and his family, was a familiar place – and a safer adventure – in Stowe. That I was pregnant with our first child only added to our anticipation of a fresh start.

It was in Vermont that my life began, with incremental steps, to take shape and direction. We weren't the only people we knew setting out for a rural life. Contemporaries were moving to Vermont and Maine and Alaska to start their own businesses, and the Stowe community was an amalgam of lifelong residents and urban refugees who moved there to ski and to build furniture, make maple syrup, paint, craft, do fine carpentry or set up rural law, dental and medical practices. Part of the ferment of the 1960s, the search for an alternative model for life was an embrace of environmental responsibility, along with a sort of "back to nature" rejection of 1950s suburbia. We wanted to turn our backs on urban expectations, grow our own vegetables, have our babies naturally, build ethical frameworks that would be good to the earth. Moving to Vermont fit that narrative very nicely, giving us a kind of ethical high ground along with the sense of adventure we felt as we drove away from Philadelphia.

With the involvement of my brother, Tom, an entrepreneur, we bought an old farmhouse that had been refitted by the previous owner to house 20 skiers in shipboard-style bunks, on the Mountain Road, the route to Stowe's famous ski area at Mount Mansfield. Learning on the fly, now with baby Katrina in a corner room on the first floor of the lodge, we served breakfast, afternoon tea, and dinner, looking up dinner recipes from the *New York Times Cookbook* and quadrupling them, learning to buy provisions from the egg man, the produce and meat suppliers, and the S.S. Pierce canned goods purveyor. In the morning, while I fed and dressed the baby, John made breakfast, setting the heat on the three-burner griddle at just the right temperature for eggs, pancakes, bacon, and sausage, on our sparkling new Garland range. Meals were served in the dining room on long trestle tables shared by guests, who could look up at murals of Viking scenes on the dining room walls, including a Nordic chatelaine, stirring a great copper pot, with a chain of keys hanging from her belt. In my mind I was that chatelaine. It was a wonderful brief period when we imagined that this would be our life. But it became clear that we were never going to support ourselves running a ski lodge that took only 20 people and accommodated them in bunk beds created for the more rugged tastes of skiers in the 1940s.

My brother, our financial partner, however, saw a great opportunity for a real estate venture, and the Stowe dream grew into a complicated project. I welcomed Tom's confidence and bold ideas, and John, acquiescing, setting aside what he might have imagined in this adventure, took on the challenge of bringing them to reality. By the end of 10 years, we had bought the inn, on 20 acres, and built 67 condominium units. In a fit of insanity, we also bought the Stowe Playhouse, with a restaurant and bar, and built an indoor tennis court, all of which was ambitious and exciting, if not exactly environmentally conscious.

After a year or so running the lodge, we began construction of condominiums on the property. By then I needed help with Katrina and hired the first of what would become a series of young women as nannies, until I met Marie Foran, the wife of a Stowe farmer, who was looking for extra income. When Erika came along, four years later, we had given up running the lodge and were managing condominium rentals and the attendant services: a swimming pool, health club, tennis court, and the other properties we had added to our businesses. I had my girls, but I was so distracted that, except for those breast-feeding months, in which I had a tactile connection to mothering, I never felt available enough to them.

The Vermont years were, in the end, a costly ten-year misadventure. John and I were diving headlong into financial ruin, and both of us were in way over our heads. The Stowe development, in addition to being too much for one naïve young couple to manage, was fatally complicated with family dynamics. I was in a business partnership with two of the most consequential men in my life. That made me feel important and meant, in theory, that I had the protection of family in my venture into business. In practice, of course, it was an impossibly stressful set up, and our timing was bad. An unstable economy in the early 1970s, and catastrophic underfinancing, at last put us into a very large financial hole.

As an anchor to windward, John stepped back from daily responsibility for the business and took a job as an insurance salesman. I was left in charge of the daily operations of the condominium rentals and the maintenance of the property, a responsibility for mechanical things I knew nothing about, for a large staff responsible for everything from making beds and plowing the roads on the property, a public relations role with our sometimes unhappy condo owners and guests. I was ill equipped, but I accepted the role. Why? Certainly hubris. Perhaps in a feminist fever, I thought I could handle it, or perhaps I wanted to defuse the tension building between my husband and my brother. In the end, I wasn't up to the job. I faced this one Saturday morning, standing in the shower, weeping, while my little girls peeked through the shower curtain, patting me and saying, "It's all right, Mommy, it's all right." It must have been a frightening scene for my children, but I felt only release and, for once, clarity. I had reached my limit.

Eventually, defeated, and with the "luxury" of being able to give up and walk away, John and I signed over our partnership to my brother who, saving us after all, pulled a few more rabbits out of his hat, left the development solvent and sold the management company to someone else. Meanwhile, we moved to Elmore, Vermont, 10 miles up a dirt road from Stowe. John was appointed to an exciting political post in the administration of Vermont Governor Tom Salmon, commuting down a country road to the state capitol in Montpelier. I took Erika to the cooperative nursery school in Stowe and enrolled Katrina in the Elmore village one-room school.

Not surprisingly, I fell into a depression. Certainly, I was humiliated by my failures in the family business we had left behind, reminded monthly by visits from the county sheriff who would deliver notices of liens against us for unpaid bills, which we would then pass on to my brother. And I felt uncertain about the future of our marriage, which had suffered from enormous strain. While seeking treatment with therapy and medication, I stenciled the walls in our bedroom, and in summer I tended a big vegetable garden, canning or freezing the produce for winter. We bought raw milk from the dairy farm next door and heated our house with wood. I learned how to bake bread and Erika and I snuggled down for afternoon naps on the couch, she with her "chubby," a favorite blanket, and me with my chubby, Erika. For money, I picked up part-time clerical work for a few hours each week. The self-sufficiency of the Elmore idyll was comforting, healing, and strengthening after the chaos we had walked away from in Stowe. We felt like pioneers. Still, alone for hours in that little house, sounds of the outdoors muffled by the cover of snow, I struggled to recover my sense of worth. I found it when I began to write.

The Vermont years, a mere 10 years of our lives, were consequential in so many ways, not the least of which was that I was an eyewitness to educational innovation there. The girls began their education in schools that sharpened my interest in education, the focus of my later career as a writer and administrator for educational organizations. A couple of years before our move, in 1973, my daughter Katrina started her education at the Stowe Cooperative Nursery School, whose founding was a creative community effort in which I took part, along with a group of parents of children aged three and four years old. At that age, our children were old enough for play-groups but too young to be enrolled at the public kindergarten in Stowe. An organizing group, mostly women, shared a book on starting a nursery school, in which we read about learning issues for four-year-olds, curriculum, creative classroom set ups with play centers and a big colorful rug for group meetings. We then found a building and, with the help of one father, a lawyer, organized a nonprofit board of directors, hired a teacher, set tuition fees, organized a schedule in which parents were required to spend time in the classroom in support of the teacher, and we opened our doors to a school that continues to exist to this day. My participation in the creation of that school was a pivotal experience for me.

The Elmore one-room school, which Katrina attended beginning in first grade, was one of the few surviving of hundreds that had once dotted the Vermont countryside. The school had been educating Elmore's rural children for genera-tions, yet it had become a contemporary experiment in education. Miss Eunice Greene the teacher to 15 children in four grades, had learned about "open classroom" teaching at an education conference. Coming home to her one-room school – literally one room – she spent a summer rearranging her classroom and curriculum to set up learning centers by subject, each with a box of three-by-five cards arranged from easiest to advanced assignments, so that children could progress in each subject on their own. The older children could help the younger ones. Each child read to Miss Greene during the day, so that she could keep track of everyone's reading ability. Miss Greene urged parents with subject matter "expertise" to come in to work with the children. I taught French, another mother played the piano and sang with the children.

I became fascinated with the school, and when a one-year term for the Elmore School Board came up, I ran for and won the seat at Town Meeting. In one consuming year, I learned a great deal about the responsibilities and limits of serving in a public office. I was not re-elected to another term – another failure on my part, this time a failure to understand my role on a public-school board, or a rural community's tolerance of change and resistance to outsiders. I also wrote my first paid nonfiction piece about the school for the *Lamoille County Weekly*. These were steps in the evolution of my career.

After I published the school story, I met Glee Kelley, a local historian who lived in a house cluttered with her collection of cut-glass vases and a mountain of newspaper clippings, in Wolcott, just down the road from Elmore. Glee, a consummate storyteller who, at 92, spent much of her time visiting her "shut-ins" in the village, was a gift to me and I to her. Her gift to me was her keen observation, her unquenchable curiosity, and her deep knowledge of the tangible history traceable down country roads. My gift to her was my hunger for her stories. Over weeks one summer, we went on daily road trips to secret places to find old country cemeteries and avenues of trees where roads used to be, and to uncover plaques marking the route Ethan Allen and his Green Mountain Boys took to meet the enemy in the American Revolution. Glee encouraged me to think of myself as a writer and to look for stories to tell. "There are acres of diamonds out there, Selby," she would say.

"Acres of diamonds."

I started writing more nonfiction articles for publication. I sold freelance pieces on political candidates, arts and sports events, profiles of local heroes, a disco dancing class, and reports of Stowe school board meetings. I earned pennies a word from the *Lamoille County Weekly, The Stowe Reporter,* then some daily papers and monthly magazines. I wrote a history of the Stowe Winter Carnival, a weeklong winter sports celebration, in a souvenir publication I put together as part of a part-time secretarial job working for the carnival's director. I wrote a profile of Glee, published in *Vermont Life* Magazine.

The Vermont years, from 1970 to 1980, were not entirely a misadventure. They also represented the years when I learned about hiring, budgeting, management, and public relations. Helping found the nursery school, writing about Katrina's one-room school, serving on the school board, reporting on school board meetings, I became interested in schools and education, and that interest would form the bedrock of my future work. I found a voice and my vocation as a writer, where I felt competent, increasingly sure of myself. In our real estate ventures, I had learned to fail utterly and get up again. And I learned that I was happiest when I had work and an independent identity in addition to being a mother and wife. In retrospect, I regret that, harassed and overextended as I was, I could not spend more time enjoying the experience of motherhood.

After his appointment in Governor Salmon's administration ended, with the end of the governor's tenure, John wanted to return to work more readily available in an urban setting. We moved to suburban Boston, Massachusetts, in 1980, where he found a new job. My own career began to fall into place, growing as my experience grew. We had very little money now, and felt some urgency to build some financial security.

Through a friend who was willing to take a chance on me based on some freelance writing clips, I became a staff writer in the communications office at Tufts University, where I became the principal reporter for its veterinary school, editor of its newsletter and publicist, selling stories about heroic dogs, wounded eagles, and breeding racehorses.

Tufts, under the leadership of its president, nutritionist Jean Mayer, was a family-friendly place to work that tolerated my absence when I was home with a sick child. But after-school coverage for the girls was a constant challenge. Like other working mothers, I struggled with childcare options for Katrina and Erika, who were then in school all day: high school girls who watched them at our house, women who ran daycare centers in their homes, neighbors who would take the girls in an emergency, all with varying success and constant guilt that I was not at home myself at the end of the school day. Erika, with the clarity of a small child, brought that home to me one harried morning when, resisting the rush to go downstairs for breakfast and school, she sat on a step halfway down the stairs. Something made me sit down beside her and ask what was wrong. Looking me straight in the eye, she said, "I don't see enough of you, Mommy." She was telling me the truth as she saw it and I knew what she was talking about. I didn't see enough of her, either. And yet, when I was at home, on days when a child was sick, I felt guilty about missing work.

John began a job selling an investment counseling service that sent him on the road. The work took him out of the office, sometimes for weeks at a time. He loved the travel, the freedom from daily supervision by a boss, and perhaps even the freedom from the daily reminders of a marriage that was falling apart. We both found independence and stability within the skeleton structure of our marriage.

Feeling more or less on my own now, except for the weekends when John was at home, I began to understand that if we were going to have the resources to send our daughters to college, I would have to earn more money. Anxious to increase my earning potential as quickly as possible, I developed the theory that as a woman in the workplace, in order to move up, I needed to move on to another job in another workplace. So, after three years at Tufts, I moved on to a regional higher education association where I was named director of communications, again with writing and editorial responsibilities, and a significant increase in salary. A couple of years later, I moved to the National Association of Independent Schools (NAIS), again boosting my salary and responsibility as communications director at a national institution. In my subsequent career, I was driven as much by fear of financial instability as I was by ambition.

NAIS is a trade association for private, nonprofit schools in the U.S. and American international schools around the world. I thrived there, writing about and promoting educational initiatives. As time went by, I lobbied to move up from a staff to an executive position, over time acquiring more staff and more and more administrative responsibility. By accident, I discovered that I was making about two-thirds the salary of my executive colleagues – a difference amounting to tens of thousands of dollars – and I went to the NAIS president to ask for an explanation and equal pay. The problem had started with my entering salary – I had been a cheaper hire than my colleagues – and was redoubled when I was promoted. I had been given a healthy increase, which pleased me, but nothing near the salary I was entitled to because, in the view of my boss, married women didn't need to earn as much as men. A new president, more conversant with the times, corrected this inequity when the whole executive staff relocated with the association to a new national location in Washington, DC.

When NAIS moved its offices to Washington, Katrina was out of college and Erika was a college freshman, and I was earning enough money to leave my marriage and move to Washington by myself. My new salary made that decision possible, but it didn't make it easy on my children, when John and I divorced and, within a few years, each of us remarried. Now that my daughters, too, are wives, mothers, and professional women, that unhappy period is, for better or worse, a piece of the history that has helped them shape their own lives.

In the move to Washington, all of the executives at NAIS became vice presidents, giving us titles to suit a new title-obsessed environment in the nation's capital, with substantial boosts in our salaries. In those years at NAIS, I learned about curriculum and leadership, school governance, accreditation, marketing and messaging, all subjects that had begun to interest me in my first exposure to education, at the Stowe Cooperative Nursery School. I felt a heightened sense of authority and personal power as I advanced through middle age.

I had one last happy job, this time inside a private school, close to stories and students and faculty, with no management responsibilities, in which I could savor stories of teaching and learning from a more intimate perspective. It was a lovely coda to my career.

My own story is an example of accidental agency, shared by opportunity and circumstance, a trajectory I share with classmates in the Vassar Class of '65. It is also, like Debby Dodds', Debbie Kolb's, and Mary Watson's, a tale of the pressure all of us were under to figure out how to have careers and manage our families at a time when neither the workplace nor the culture was helping us to make that possible.

Local and national legislation and cultural expectations have helped to improve work and family balance issues in the 50 years since we struggled to make it all work. Parental leave for both fathers and mothers is provided in some workplaces. Daycare is a part of the culture both at the workplace and in the community; public schools have after-school programs that keep children safe while their parents put in eight-hour days and more. Parents routinely string together summer day-camp programs when their children are out of school. But it's still hard, and the pressure to find balance still rests heavily on young parents. And parents find themselves moderating or resetting their career ambitions, at least during the years when their children are small. We started the effort but there is much still to be done.

CHAPTER 8

Stepping into a Man's World

"Work was exciting, heady. I had to readjust to the fact that I took myself very seriously in the workplace. I thrived on it, loved it."

From the Bank Street conversations

Eighty-five percent of my classmates spent a significant portion of their adult lives in the workplace. Nevertheless, we felt frustrated, because the workplace did not welcome us as women. Most of us just walked through doors as they seemed to open a crack, following, as we had in college, the subject matter that interested us. Some classmates plunged fearlessly into a world propelled by profit and dominated by men and, with luck and hard work and against many barriers, built successful careers.

We faced routine, everyday sex discrimination, a major barrier to women, everywhere in the workplace in the 1960s and 1970s. Gender discrimination affected everything – office networking, salaries, inclusion in decision making, opportunities for advancement. For example, when jobs opened up for Mary Watson, our classmate who excelled in corporate sales, she was unafraid to step into them. But that didn't make her immune to the roadblocks that were constantly in front of her. When she joined International Paper, a Fortune 500 company, as director of new product development, "Men hit on us all the time, it was just part of the work experience," she says. Mary found that male colleagues would deliberately schedule important meetings when she was out of the office, traveling, or home with a child. And she soon discovered that she was not paid what men in the same position earned. Nonetheless, Mary became a valued member of International Paper's marketing team, so much so that her superior, nervous that the company might lose her, asked the president, "What are you going to do about Mary?" The next day Mary learned that she had been made a vice president of the firm. Her salary, however, did not change with her new title.

Soon Mary was offered a job at a competing private marketing firm. By this time, she knew what the men with her responsibilities were being paid, and what she was worth. She asked for an appropriate salary and got it, and she left International Paper for the new job. "I was not political at Vassar, and I'm not sure I was fully aware of discrimination against women until I faced it myself in the workplace. I learned, finally, to stand up for myself," she says, "and I have encouraged my daughter to insist on equal pay for her work."

"American Women," the report of the Kennedy Commission in the early 1960s, which raised the specter of sex discrimination, may have had a direct influence on Congress, when Title VII of the Civil Rights Act of 1964 decided to include "sex," or gender, in its language forbidding discrimination. In that landmark legislation, Title VII was written to prohibit employment discrimination based on race, color, religion, sex and national origin. Some contend that mentioning discrimination on the basis of sex in the bill was a kind of a joke – a way to discourage male congressmen from passing the bill. Nevertheless, it was this inclusion of gender in the language of the act that enabled classmate, *Newsweek* editor Lynn Povich and her colleagues to pursue the first sex discrimination lawsuit to be undertaken by women in the media, in 1970.

In her book *The Good Girls Revolt*, published in 2012, Lynn tells the story of how she and the women she worked with at *Newsweek* saw an opening to file a sex discrimination complaint against the magazine. This is another tale of the Class of '65 on the cusp of change.

At the time we were coming out of college, *Newsweek* (and other newsmagazines) hired young women, just out of college, in starting jobs in the mail room, as fact checkers on the news staff, or sometimes, if they were lucky, as researcher/reporters, whose notes would be passed on to the writers for their articles. Young women aspiring to be writers took these jobs in the hope that they would be promoted. Young men just out of college, with the same credentials, that is, a college degree from a good school, would be given those writing jobs right away. As time went by, many women, including researchers, would find that they were handing their notes to men who were brand new college graduates with less *Newsweek* experience than they had. The articles were written under the men's bylines. This was "just the way it was," Lynn says, "and we all accepted it."

Until they didn't. Reminded by a friend that the language of the 1964 Civil Rights law included discrimination against women, one staffer, Judy Gingold, began to think about whether *Newsweek*'s hiring system was legal. She talked to the Equal Employment Opportunities Commission (EEOC), the agency created to enforce the Title VII provisions of the 1964 Civil Rights Act. EEOC confirmed that it was illegal and, after that, Judy told a colleague, who talked to other colleagues, all in secret, in the ladies' room or outside the office. Soon there were 46 women who wanted to right what was wrong with the *Newsweek* system. Lynn writes, "With great trepidation, we decided to take on what we saw as a massive injustice: a segregated system of journalism that divided research, reporting, writing, and editing roles solely on the basis of gender."

Lynn was in a unique position relative to the lawsuit. Her boss, the editor of the Life and Leisure section for which Lynn was reporting, liked her work and encouraged her to try out as a writer for the section, which meant that at the time of the discrimination suit, she had broken the barrier to women seeking writing jobs.

In 1970, with the guidance of a young American Civil Liberties Union (ACLU) lawyer, Eleanor Holmes Norton, the 46 women employees of *Newsweek* filed a complaint with the EEOC charging that women at *Newsweek* were "systematically discriminated against in both hiring and promotion and forced to assume a subsidiary role," Povich explains. And their timing was exquisite. They filed suit just as *Newsweek* was publishing its first cover story on the women's movement – "Women in Revolt" – which meant that their complaint got a lot of coverage in other papers and magazines, and *Newsweek* was left in a very awkward position. That action and a subsequent one two years later effectively changed the *Newsweek* hiring system in favor of hiring men and women on an equal footing, and the *Newsweek* women's example prompted similar suits among women in media at Time Inc., NBC, *Reader's Digest*, the *Washington Post*, the *New York Times* and a number of other publications over the next few years.

In 1975, five years after the suit had been filed, Ed Kosner, the new Editor-in-Chief, asked Lynn, after 10 years at *Newsweek* and six as a writer, to try out as the first female senior editor of the magazine. She decided to try editing and found that she loved it, more than writing. She was doing well working with writers but, she says, "What proved more daunting was being the only woman in the story meetings. Despite Ed's support, it was clear that most of the editors didn't take me seriously. In a room filled with testosterone and egotism, I had to learn to speak up and defend my stories and my writers."

"For most of us middle-class ladies," Lynn writes, "standing up for our rights marked the first time we had done anything political or feminist. It would be the radicalizing act that gave us the confidence and the courage to find ourselves and stake our claim."

My experience was in the relatively less pressured non-profit world, an environment more tolerant of women in administration. Some classmates plunged fearlessly into a man's world and, with luck and grit, and against many barriers, built successful careers. Classmates Moira Burke and Dede Thompson Bartlett are two of those intrepid women. Moira, in becoming a physician, was entering a field that, while not closed to women, was certainly not welcoming, especially to those women who also planned to have families. Her journey into medicine was driven by pure grit and determination. Dede's rise to the top of the corporate pyramid "didn't happen logically," as she put it. At each juncture on her career path, she followed her interests and curiosity and, with serendipity and a little help, she kept walking through doors until she was the only woman at the top in two very large American companies.

Sex discrimination was particularly ruthless in the overworked, exhausted fraternity of physicians in training. The presence of so many women in medicine now is heartening, and a tribute to women, like Moira, who came before.

The Ophthalmologist: Moira's Story

Unlike many of us, Moira Burke's vision for her life was not limited by 1950s norms and expectations for women. Moira had a plan. By the time she was in fourth grade, she knew she wanted to be a doctor. A determined red-haired girl, she was not dissuaded from her ambitions by the low social expectations of women during her childhood. Instead, she found barriers to *opportunities* for women. She faced – and faced down – obstacles at every turn in her chosen career. By moving forward in medicine, against all odds, Moira really served as a pioneer, but she didn't set out to be one. "I never had any sense of myself as a feminist, then," Moira says. "I just know that I was driven."

Looking back now, Moira remembers that her parents, burdened with work and money issues – like all our parents, coming out of the Depression – lived with disappointment about their lives. Moira was surrounded by adults with thwarted ambitions, and she was determined to have a better life. In high school, she applied for admission to Buffalo Seminary, a girls' private school, but the school turned down her application for a scholarship. That, too, set her determination to defy expectations of her and "show the world I was different!" she says. She was headed for medicine.

Why medicine? Perhaps because of her mother's chronic health issues, perhaps because it was in her genes. Moira did not discover until her graduation from medical school that she was, in fact, fulfilling her father's ambition. He had intended to go to medical school himself, he confessed, but he had set aside his own plans in order to help his brother and two sisters go to college. Later he would work toward a doctoral degree in science but would never complete his dissertation. Moira's aunt on her mother's side had gone to nursing school. Moira was naturally drawn to science and mathematics, and was a very good student. Even in high school, her extracurricular activities were science-oriented. Every summer, Moira earned a National Science Foundation Scholarship to participate in a summer study program researching cancer at Roswell Park Cancer Institute in Buffalo.

Moira tells another story of her father's own thwarted plans and his concern that she had realistic, achievable goals. Sophomore Father's Weekend, a Vassar tradition then, in which sophomores invited their fathers to be their "dates" during a weekend of activities, provided an opportunity for Moira and her father to have more significant talks. "I was seriously doubting my intellectual strength at that time," she says, "and he was supportive, urging me to keep on plugging, but he suggested that I consider professional alternatives, like, for example, pharmacy."

In her senior year at Vassar, wasting no time, Moira applied to five medical schools, while telling no one, except the professors writing recommendations, just in case she was not accepted. Though advised during her admission interviews that it would be difficult for her to be accepted at medical school (because she was a woman), Moira was accepted at all five schools. She chose the medical school near home, at the University of Buffalo. Moira was one of only nine women in her class, out of 90 classmates. Despite routine harassment, cleavage evaluations by their male classmates and dismissive regard from faculty, Moira notes that the women's academic performance put them in the top 30 percent of the class.

It was at the University of Buffalo that Moira met Brian Murphy, a dental student, and they married at the end of their second year. Thinking of her earlier summer studies with National Science foundation scholarships, Moira at first thought she would focus on hematology and oncology, but in her last two years, she began to specialize in ophthalmology, a specialty that, looking ahead, presented an opportunity to build a more flexible practice. Ophthalmology was interesting as a kind of general practice for one human organ because it enabled the doctor to see and treat patients of all ages, whole families from children to grandparents. And ophthalmology was a medical, surgery, and preventative practice, providing lots of variety – and it was lucrative. It could support her, and later, when she was a single mother, her children.

Following graduation from medical school, Brian and Moira together went in search of internships and residencies, interviewing at a prestigious university, where the ophthalmology department chair told Moira, "You have an outstanding résumé, but we really don't take women as interns. However, I can tell you how to get in," he added, jotting down the name of a hotel and a room number.

Moira and Brian settled in Philadelphia for their internships. Because she knew she wanted to pursue ophthalmology and, for complicated reasons, to get herself into the right training cohort of men, she was required to apply early for a residency at the prestigious Wills Eye Institute in Philadelphia. Wills, established in 1832, is the oldest continuously operating eye clinic and hospital in the country. She was accepted for this residency, a coup, in advance of her internship, and her place was held for her. Ophthalmology is a lucrative practice, which makes its training particularly competitive, and Wills was among the best places to train.

Meanwhile, Moira interned at Lankenau Hospital, like other interns, in three other specialties, in addition to ophthalmology – pediatrics, neurology, and medicine. Serendipitously, one of the medical residents at Lankenau was a woman she had met during her high school summer studies at Roswell Park Cancer Institute. That woman, Bonnie Dorwart, became Moira's only mentor, helping her to negotiate the challenges of a new doctor at Lankenau.

Looking back on those years, she remembers a remarkable

experience that reinforces her belief in the powerful and healing personal connections that are available to a physician. "I had been taking care of a little girl suffering from hydro-cephalus during my pediatric rotation," she says, "and I saw her again on my neurology rotation. The child had a shunt in her brain that had become infected, and we needed to inject an antibiotic directly into her ventricle – a challenging proce-dure, and antibiotics were not as effective then as they are now."

"I had to make the injection. I had gotten very close to the family, and it was heartbreaking to all of us when the antibiotic did not work, and the child died," Moira continues. "Then, on the last day of my internship, in June, I was called on the hospital pager to find that the little girl's family had left me a gift, a small Hummel figurine that still sits on a shelf in my house. It was the most poignant moment of my career."

"That's what medicine is all about," Moira says.

When she began her residency at Wills Eye Institute, Moira was the only woman resident in her year (one woman had been accepted the year before and one would be accepted the next year). At Wills, Moira continued to overcome the obsta-cles in place for the women residents, who were, among other things, not supplied with sleeping rooms for use during night-time "on call" assignments. They were not able to use the library at the hospital, as it was located on the floor where the men were provided with beds.

Despite having been warned not to get pregnant during her residency ("you will not have children" was in the fine print of her contract), Moira found herself pregnant with an unplanned child. Colleagues advised her not to tell anyone she was pregnant until her fifth month, using Velcro to expand the waistline of her clothing, to delay as long as possible any awareness of her condition. Male colleagues, exhausted by the punishing schedule and resentful at further proof that women were not suited to be doctors, let her know that they would be unwilling to cover for her should she go into labor on an "on call" night. Why should they, they thought, when they were already working so hard, and she shouldn't have gotten pregnant anyway? And, given that residents had one week vacation for every year of their three-year residency, Moira was informed that she would have to use her three weeks' total vacation for a three-week postpartum break with her newborn. She remembers, "I performed five cataract surgeries on the day I gave birth to my son Brendan."

Moira and Brian next moved to Florida, settling finally in Tampa, where Brian was able to buy into a dental surgery. Moira, then pregnant with her second son, Ryan, had difficulty joining an existing ophthalmology practice. As a woman, and a mother of two boys, she was someone whom practitioners believed "would not be able to pull her own weight" as a practice partner. The alternative was to set up her own practice, but for that, Moira needed to rent an office – a $25,000 annual expense for one room, with one employee. Banks then were unwilling to loan funds to women unless a man was willing to cosign the loan. Brian signed, but since he was in a different practice, the bank was still unwilling to loan her money, suggesting that she drum up business until she had enough money to invest in an office. For several months, Moira practiced at home, setting up an examination room in her garage with a split lamp and other minimal equipment for eye exams, and she worked in other doctor's offices when there was time and space available. In the beginning, her practice grew from workmen's compensation referrals – patients whose eyes were injured on the job – from other ophthalmologists.

In 30 years, staying quietly under the radar, she built a practice of 15,000 patients. "I wanted to show those guys who said I couldn't carry my own weight!" she says. "I invested my personality in my practice," she adds, "developing relation-ships with my patients over time, just as if it were a general practice and I was their primary care physician. One of the best parts about ophthalmology," she explains, "is that it's possible to develop long-term relationships with families. Patients came back every year, and soon new generations of the same families."

About the time Moira had built up enough of a practice, and some collateral, to borrow the necessary funds and take a three-year lease, Brian announced that he was unhappy in his practice and with their marriage, and left Tampa. Moira was faced with the challenge of balancing medicine and mother-hood, now as a single parent with school-aged children. For Moira, too, childcare was a constant challenge.

Eventually, Moira was recruited by the University of South Florida (USF) to teach cataract surgery in a clinical setting, taking a day a week from her own practice. That allowed her to be a part of the ongoing changes in medicine, and particu-larly ophthalmology, resulting from medical innovations over the years. To emphasize the changes that have taken place, and the necessity for doctors to keep training throughout their practice, she notes, "There is nothing I did at the end of my career that I learned at Wills Eye Institute. It was all new." In 2016, Moira was given the "Remarkabull Woman" award by the University of South Florida, referencing its mascot, the bull, and recognizing her dedication to her profession and years of service to the Tampa community.

Then, concerned that with the growth of HMOs, the ability to work in private practice might disappear, Moira joined the Air Force Reserve in the early 1990s as a hedge against what might happen to her own practice in the future. Through the Air Force, Moira could earn the continuing education credits she needed to stay current in her profession, and it seemed unlikely that as a reservist she would be called into active duty.

That proved to be a wrong assumption. When Desert Storm heated up in the early 1990s, the medical staff at Andrews Air Force Base in Maryland was deployed to Germany, and reservists were left to care for Desert Storm cases at Andrews. While she was deployed at Andrews, a friend moved into Moira's home in Florida to care for her youngest son, Ryan, who was still in high school.

A brief second marriage that "was not good for the kids" ended in divorce, and Moira remained single until, at 64, she met the man she calls "the love of my life," Bernie Hochberg, and married him. Bernie, a child of the Holocaust and a widower who had raised four boys by himself was ill, so after six years, Moira decided to retire from her practice in order to spend time traveling and enjoying life with him. After Bernie died, in 2012, Moira went back to work in another doctor's office, prepping patients for surgery and doing post-operative work. Today, Moira still keeps her hand in, reviewing charts and doing third party administrative work for the Veterans Administration, helping to address the nightmares presented by the insurance industry. Moira hopes that the insurance industry will eventually go to a "single payer" system, but meanwhile she loves the VA and values the opportunity to help them "do the things that should be done for patients." She retired in the fall of 2020, at age 77, 51 years after graduating from medical school, to have more time to be with her grandchildren and immerse herself in the cultural life of Tampa.

What is she proudest of? "My resilience," Moira says.

The Corporate Executive: Dede's Story

In the fall of 2020, in celebration of the centennial of women's franchise, Dede Thompson Bartlett was interviewed by the

New Canaan Museum and Historical Society as part of a series on 19 women leaders in New Canaan. How, the interviewer wanted to know, did Dede's extraordinary career happen, making her the most powerful, and only, woman in the executive suite at two major American companies? In that interview, Dede describes herself as a late bloomer. An only child living in the thrum of New York City, and the only child of only children raised in the Depression, she learned early the family values of independence, self-reliance and hard work most carefully nourished in the Thompson household. That only begins to explain how she found herself at the top of the corporate pyramid at Mobil Oil and Philip Morris, two companies in the Fortune 500 listing of the largest and most successful American companies, 40 years later.

Dede, who through the years has remained tall and slim and a traditional sparkling-eyed American beauty, remembers that they were a very focused family, and education was "job one." Mr. Thompson had two jobs – in the daytime as a naval research scientist and in the evening as an adjunct professor at Brooklyn Poly Technic Institute (now part of New York University) – in order to send Dede to private New York City schools and to college. Her mother, whose own father had refused to send her to college, trained her focus on Dede's education. Concerned that Dede was not getting enough challenging work, she pulled her out of Garden Country Day School and enrolled her in Spence, an all-girls school where she would get a more rigorous education.

Dede knew how to apply herself to academic work, and she did well at Vassar, focusing on a French major that would get her on a Junior Year Abroad program to France, though history really interested her more. "I would go to college, work for two years (because you never knew what might happen and you might have to fall back on some profession later on in life) and then get married," Dede says. She planned, after working a couple of years, to "marry a guy who went to one of the Ivies and would be a good provider," she explains. "My job was to be a good help mate in his career and raise the children well."

At the end of senior year, she was about to be engaged to a man who had gone to Princeton on a Marine Corps scholarship, who was on his way to Vietnam. They decided to defer a formal engagement and marriage until he had returned from the war. Instead, she hung around New York, going to a lot of parties but unable to find a good job. "My life was aimless," Dede says. Seeking to help her daughter find focus and structure, Mrs. Thompson took her down to NYU, which at the time did not require graduate records exams and, on the spot, Dede enrolled in a master's degree program in American history. Her mother was right. "It was one of the best decisions I ever made," she says.

If she was a late bloomer, it was NYU that got her going. "NYU was a great awakening," she says, "offering a culture radically different to that at Vassar – gritty, tough, diverse, sometimes hostile, and challenging." While she was getting her master's degree, Dede found a job doing research at the nonprofit Far East America Council, an organization that produced programs to bring business leaders together from countries around the Pacific Rim. That enabled her to pay her tuition in full at NYU, going to night classes over three years. When she wasn't studying, she was going out every night, in the thick of a "heady" culture of social unrest, partly over the Vietnam War, which was becoming increasingly unpopular as it dragged on and more and more young people were drawn into it by the draft.

When her boyfriend came home from the war in 1967, they became engaged and plunged into plans for a wedding, but both found themselves much changed by the experiences each had had during the two years they were separated. He'd had a rough time in the war, and Dede's world had opened up. Dede asked her mother to meet her for lunch, and told her she felt unhappy about her impending marriage and thought she wanted to break the engagement. Her mother understood. "I will take care of canceling all the wedding arrangements," she said, "but you must do two things yourself. You must tell him right away, and you must return the engagement ring and the string of pearls he bought you while in Asia."

"I felt so free, so relieved, having made that decision," Dede says, "and I was so grateful to my mother for her support. I decided then that I wanted to be that kind of mother."

Luck opened a door for Dede. Shortly before she had completed her master's degree at NYU in 1969, Dede met a woman, who has since become a good friend. She worked in public relations and saw Dede's potential as a PR person. This friend took her "very slim" résumé around to people at her public relations agency, Ruder & Finn. This led to Dede's career breakthrough. But it came at a price. She got the job and she got the clients no one else wanted – gray goods dealers in the garment district, a Miami real estate firm and a steel pipe manufacturer in St. Louis. She remembers going to work in her "pink Tricia Nixon dress" and up what was "practically a hand crank elevator" to her office. Her boss was also a character, a scruffy ex-newspaper editor who kept a scotch bottle at the ready in the lower right-hand drawer of his desk. As Dede described it, "The two of us were quite a pair: I looked like Mary Tyler Moore, and he was the spitting image of Ed Asner."

"But by accident, I found work that I was good at, public relations," she goes on. "And that ignited a passion in me for my work."

In 1972, after three years at Ruder & Finn, Dede had achieved enough of a professional profile that she was recruited to be director of corporate communications, and then – at

27 – a vice president at a "hot shot electronics company," Bowmar Instrument Corporation, which produced the first electronic calculator, dubbed the Bowmar Brain. Now she found herself quoted in all the financial media. It was a heady time. The experience of receiving her first year-end corporate bonus and stock options in the company was "astonishing" she says. She had money and recognition and it was intoxicating. Dede rented an apartment off Fifth Avenue in New York City and began to feel very independent and self-sufficient.

"I figured out where I wanted to go. I enjoyed working, felt good at what I did, found the work challenging, interesting, with both monetary and psychological rewards." Her mother's lessons in self-reliance had paid off in a confident, self-assured young professional. Though there was no particular man in her life, Dede wanted children and now it occurred to her that she had enough resources to take care of herself and someone else. Perhaps she should adopt. Then Jim Bartlett came along, "a great guy from Colorado, with a fine mind and a good sense of humor, working in the financial services industry in New York. Jim was the icing on the cake," Dede says. They married in 1974 when Dede was 30 years old.

Shortly afterwards, Bowmar's financial troubles became front page news and the company declared bankruptcy. Dede notes that its meteoric rise and fall made it the topic of a case study at the Harvard Business School. In her next job, she would find a company with a strong balance sheet. And in her search, she found a job at the eminently financially stable Mobil Oil Corporation, where she began as a communications executive.

As a PR professional, she was in charge of state government relations, and then moved on to stints in employee relations, lobbying, affirmative action and corporate governance. "It was a transformative experience," she says. Mobil Corporation was short of women at the executive level, but it had a strong career development operation, in which employees were advanced based on potential. Within a few years, Dede was named president of the Mobil Foundation, its grant making arm, and became Corporate Secretary, the person at the right hand of the board chair. The Mobil Foundation made grants of $15 million to arts, health, and civic organizations, awarding small grants to a number of programs. As the foundation president, Dede was chair of its contributions committee, vetting grant requests.

It was the board chair and CEO of Mobil, himself the father of four daughters, who had mentored Dede. Conversations with his daughters helped him to see the importance of advancing women at Mobil. Dede was, she says, "the direct beneficiary of the women's movement." As Corporate Secretary, Dede was responsible for investor relations, corporate filings involving Mobil's 950 subsidiary corporations, stocks, and managing the work of the board of directors. She now advises young women going into the corporate world to "arm yourself with quantitative skills. I had to learn them on the fly."

She was very fortunate, but along the way, Dede admits, there were plenty of hurdles. "First, I was thrilled to be the highest ranking woman at Mobil, but frankly, I never liked being the only woman in the room." The routine "alpha stuff," the belligerent behavior, interruptions and out-talking that men use in their interactions is abated when there is a critical mass of women in the room. As the only woman, Dede had to learn to articulate and defend her ideas, holding her own in discussions, keeping it civil. Working at the executive level also required a different kind of engagement. "In the beginning of our careers, we could be the cute ingenues to get air time. In middle age, in the executive suite, I had to deliver substance to be heard."

At the beginning of her marriage, Dede had successfully

settled herself in a new job. The biggest challenge and the biggest culture shock she had to face came two years after she was married, in 1976, when she and Jim moved to New Canaan, Connecticut. They had looked into buying a coop in New York, but Jim felt that coops were not a good financial investment. Dede began to understand how profoundly different their ideas were about where to live. Jim was a Coloradan, used to great outdoor spaces, and Dede was a lifelong New Yorker. New Canaan was in commuting distance to New York City, so they both could continue at their jobs, but for Dede, the Connecticut suburbs were a foreign country. "All my life, I had never lived in a house. I didn't know how to drive! There were no restaurants in town, and the women shopped for groceries in their tennis clothes with pompoms on their sneakers." She adds, "As the children came along, there were no real support systems. Stores weren't open past five p.m., and not at all on Sundays." Dede shopped and cooked all the family meals on weekends.

When the Welcome Wagon woman dropped by wearing a mop cap with a basket on her arm, she came into Dede's living room and spread out samples of all kinds of household products. "She told me about the Newcomers Club," Dede says, "and I asked if I could bring my husband. Wrong question. I went to the first meeting and their major project was to paint mailboxes. I thought, 'Where am I?'"

Her first five years in New Canaan were tough, but for Jim it was easy, so she told herself, "I've got to make this work." But she had no role models for this transition. Their first child, Katie, was born in 1977, and their second, Jay, in 1980. Working part-time was not an option for Dede, given her responsibilities at Mobil, so she had to be creative at finding live-in childcare that would be there for the children when she caught the 7:30 a.m. commuter train with Jim in the morning. "A friend had found a perfect Mary Poppins nanny," she says, "but I did not. Some of the helpers were lovely people – a young Mormon woman on her work year comes to mind – I am still in touch with her. Some of the nannies were good and some were immature, but we limped along." She admits that those years were not easy for anyone, including her children.

When her children were growing up, they were the focus of Dede's life. In an interview with Dede for her book *Mothers on the Fast Track,* classmate Mary Ann Mason notes that throughout her time at Mobil, Dede had managed to be home by 6:30, in order to have dinner with her children. Family activities revolved around summers in Nantucket and Martha's Vineyard and winter weekends on the ski slopes. She spent most of her vacation in taking days off to attend her children's school events. However, being one of the few working mothers in the town was not always easy on her or her children. "There were three other women on the commuter train in the morning, and we all became close. Our children were in the same preschool, and we created a bond." These women were, she says, "not the country club set," but they were her tribe.

A feeling of belonging in New Canaan came in time, and the proof is that in the 40 years she has lived there, Dede has involved herself in the community, as Clerk of Session in the Presbyterian Church, and as founder of the New Canaan Domestic Violence Partnership. Her path to domestic violence as an issue grew out of her professional work.

When Mobil moved its offices to Virginia in 1990, Dede chose not to relocate with them. Her family was settled in Connecticut so she needed to find new work. She feared she would never be able to work at that level of senior management again. However, Philip Morris, which was located two blocks from Mobil's headquarters in midtown Manhattan, recruited her to be Vice President and Corporate Secretary – again a tribute to her extraordinary professional profile. The move to a tobacco company involved some serious conversation with her children about smoking. Even the conglomerate's food products presented a challenge. She told her son and daughter that Philip Morris also produced Velveeta Cheese through its Kraft Foods business. "Velveeta Cheese is a $200 million business," she told her children. "And although we don't buy it, we're not going to say anything bad about Velveeta!"

Corporate secretaries are usually lawyers, whose role is to protect the board. When the law suits against tobacco companies became more intense in the mid-1990s, the company decided that Dede's job should be in the hands of another lawyer. Dede understood that decision, but she had a problem with how they handled her in the process, shifting her, without consultation, to another area of the company, in a role that did not fit. "I negotiated an arrangement to stay on at the company," she says, devoting her time to social and philanthropic programs at Philip Morris. One of the cornerstones of that arrangement was a program she developed to raise awareness about domestic violence and to encourage companies to develop programs to help their employees who were victims of domestic violence. Why domestic violence? It was another serendipitous accident, a door that opened as a result of Dede's networking efforts. Ellie Guggenheimer, an older friend and New York force of nature, who had discovered and adopted her, no doubt seeing her promise, called Dede to ask a favor. "Ellie wanted to know if I could find a meeting space in Philip Morris's big midtown building for the New York Domestic Violence Council, one of her philanthropies, and I said 'Sure.'" That meeting, which Dede attended, so captured Dede's attention that she pulled together a group of colleagues from other companies to develop the first-ever conference on domestic violence issues, asking the question, "What do companies need to know to protect women – including our own employees – from domestic abuse?" Suddenly, Philip Morris was in charge of a "blue ribbon operation," Dede says, and on the side of social justice.

Dede began a phase of her professional and personal life in which she focused on important issues for the benefit of women, becoming another midwife to initiatives improving the lives of women. It was a program in which Philip Morris, now called Altria, invested in the community, at the same time encouraging a positive public profile for the corporation.

The subject of physical and sexual abuse was new to Dede, though sexual harassment was familiar territory. "I can't remember a time when I wasn't propositioned in the work-place," she says. "I learned to work around it, and I learned not to let it attack my self-confidence. You don't want to think you only got your job because you were attractive." Dede notes that her male colleagues also stepped in to help fend off unwanted attention.

It was Ellie who brought Dede into the Women's Forum of New York. This is a "premier organization," quoting Dede, of 7,500 women worldwide, who are engaged in the professions, arts, and philanthropy. Dede would later serve as president of the Women's Forum of New York and a former chair of the advisory board of the National Domestic Violence Hotline, and for those efforts she has earned many awards.

Dede took early retirement at 58. Mary Ann Mason reports in her interview for her book, noted earlier, that Dede found the work environment at Philip Morris "included higher pressure and longer hours. The level and pace of the work changed," Dede told Mary Ann. "Philip Morris was a much more aggressive company ... it was really getting be tough to balance work and family." At this point, her family took priority.

It was time, she said. "The work I had started on domestic violence had become a nationally recognized $250 million program. On the personal side, our daughter was getting married, our son was graduating from college, and we were building a new house in New Canaan. The time was ripe for me to move on to the next chapter."

The lessons of creating the domestic violence initiative "taught me that I was not afraid to start new things. It was exciting!" she adds. Dede took what she had learned at Philip Morris and committed herself to work in a volunteer capacity to protect victims of domestic violence, beginning with creating the New Canaan Domestic Violence Partnership, with partners in five Fairfield County, Connecticut towns. Each of these towns developed similar organizations using the template Dede had helped create in New Canaan.

Dede was asked by the interviewer for the New Canaan Museum, "What advice do you give young women going into business?" Besides advising them to hone their quantitative skills, Dede encourages young women to create networks in the business community. In addition, she warned, "Bad things will happen in your career. There will be roadblocks to your advancement, and you may even, at some point, be fired. The key is how you manage those roadblocks, how you reinvent yourself. One of the best jobs I ever had was a job – developing philanthropic programs – that I invented."

Back in the dark ages at Vassar, when women weren't expected to look for career advice, my classmates and I went to Mrs. Johnson in the Vocational Bureau and she advised us to try the Radcliffe secretarial program. Remembering that, and in an extraordinary act of generosity to Vassar, Dede and her husband Jim have donated $10 million for the construction on the Vassar campus of The Dede Thompson Bartlett Center, which will house the admission and career education offices. Over the past 10 years, Dede has funded paid internships to Vassar students to help them start their careers.

Moira and Dede broke into men's occupations, focusing on work in addition to their domestic spheres, and giving back to their communities at the same time. Other classmates have also worked hard to benefit their communities, outside of the workplace. Hope Oliker Hageman, whose story comes next, is one of those women.

CHAPTER 9

Volunteering from the Home Front

"You can have a lot of irons and a lot of fires and really make some progress, and that gives me a great sense of accomplishment. I never expected to be this busy, all the time, 24 hours a day, and it feels good if it's going well on a lot of fronts."

The Bank Street conversations

I n an era on the cusp of transformation for women, when friends were tipping over the cusp and going out to find work and establish careers, a smaller cohort of women from the Class of '65 had traditional lives as homemakers, wives, and mothers. Some of them worked for a few years, until children came along, then stayed home to focus on their families, defining themselves principally in relation to their husbands, their children, and their homes. Often identifying themselves laughingly as "dinosaurs" at class reunions, they have filled their lives with the work of running a household, volunteer responsibilities, and sometimes a creative pursuit – painting, gardening, or some other artistic expression. Another larger cohort stayed at home while raising children, then returned to the workplace to develop a career in midlife. At least one classmate did the opposite, building a career in banking until, in her 40s, she married and gave birth to a daughter that, to her great surprise, she didn't want to leave in order to continue her career. Instead, she left the job that had been waiting for her.

Classmate Ruth Levy Perles had earned a master's degree as a reading specialist at Columbia University before she and her husband Henry, a lawyer, married in 1968. Moving from New York City, they bought a house in Easton, a suburban Connecticut town, near Westport, where Henry set up his own law office. Ruth, who had been teaching children with learning differences at a New York private school, was soon hired by "an incredible woman," a director of special education in the Westport school system, who took Ruthie, though she did not have a special education degree, on the basis of her credentials. "But because of my Vassar degree! She trusted that I would figure out what to do even though I had never taken special ed courses."

"I was lucky all along the way," she adds, "with support and encouragement from Westport school administrators." Ruth taught until a month before her oldest son, Josh, was born. It was then that she became a full-time wife and mother.

"It just kind of happened, I sort of drifted into a traditional life," Ruth says. "It was what I expected to do with my life." Ruth's mother, who had been a child study major at Vassar, was restless in her role as mother and housekeeper. Remembering that her mother would defer to her to set a pretty dinner table, a task that didn't interest Mrs. Levy, Ruth wanted to invest herself enthusiastically in that role. "In my neighborhood, I was surrounded by women who were also at home, raising their families. They became my close friends." It was only when college friends drifted the other way, into careers, that she sometimes felt guilty and "apologetic," she says, "that I was living a life that involved less stress and pressure." Still relying on her training as a reading specialist, Ruthie spent the next 40 years volunteering as a tutor in inner-city schools, "trying to get kids on grade level by third grade."

Ruth and Henry had the gift of a common vision for their lives. Both were interested in decorating and design, in creating a beautiful house, and more importantly, they had agreed when they married that when children came, Ruth would stay at home, managing the household and childcare and curating a stunning garden. Her mentor was Henry's mother, Blanche, a style maven, who throughout their marriage urged Ruthie to "trust your instincts. You have a wonderful eye for color and design."

"I understand that I was lucky," Ruthie says, "to be able to make that choice. Henry gave me that choice." She goes on. "Henry liked the arrangement, because he wanted to come home to what I could provide – a glass of wine, a good meal, a clean house, the children picked up from school. And I love to provide that." Thinking of her own daughter-in-law, raising two boys and working full-time in New York, she adds, "Now, most women can't choose, they have to work to help bring in enough income to raise their families."

Classmate Hope Oliker Hageman tells a similar story of not exactly *deciding* not to pursue a career as other classmates were doing. Hope, whose domestic responsibilities included those of a corporate wife, with social obligations that made her a partner in her husband's career, also speaks of being "sidetracked," she says, trading paid work for cultural experiences that were shaped around her husband's career, but tapped into her own interests in international cultural exchange. "If I had had a career, it probably would have been in journalism,"

Hope says. "Work permits in other countries, though, got in the way, and my volunteer activities all had less to do with writing and more to do with making a difference in people's lives, and I found that rewarding."

International Corporate Wife: Hope's Story

Statuesque with laughing eyes, and drawn to color in her clothes and surroundings, Hope Hageman says her embrace of diverse cultures began with a book she read and reread when she was a little girl, visiting her grandmother. At six years old, just learning to read, Hope came upon the book, *Child Life in All Lands*, on a bookshelf, and she asked her grandmother if she could take it home with her. The answer was "yes." The next Christmas, Santa Claus added a second book, *Children of Other Lands,* a big book with beautiful illustrations of costumed children and landscapes from around the world, to Hope's library. Both books, with worn covers and tattered bindings, are still in Hope's possession, reminding her of her fascination with other cultures that began when she was a child.

It's a good thing that Hope and Alvin Hageman found each other, because Alvin, the son of a career Army officer, had spent a lot of his childhood overseas and shared Hope's interest in the rest of the world. They had known each other since high school in Auburn, New York. Alvin was the tallest boy in dancing class, she says. When Hope graduated, Alvin was already in Malawi. She spent the summer working as a reporter for a daily newspaper in upstate New York, where she had had summer jobs in college, and saving money to buy a plane ticket to Central Africa. There, over their parents' objections, they would marry.

At the end of the summer, Hope flew to Central Africa with

her wedding dress in her suitcase. There, while Alvin worked at the cotton cooperative in Chiromo, a small town in the south of Malawi, Hope found a job in Blantyre, a commercial hub, as a reporter for the *Malawi Times*, a bi-weekly paper that was a part of the global syndicate of papers owned by Fleet Street newspaper magnate Lord Roy Thomson. "I somehow managed to parlay my 'experience' in New York into a reporting job there," Hope notes.

While Hope was still in the U.S., Alvin had asked a Belgian priest, whom he knew as a beer drinking companion at the general store, to preside over their marriage. The men now arranged a beautiful wedding in a small church in the Elephant Swamp in Chiromo. Hope, fearless as she always was, says she was not nervous at all on the day of her wedding. "It wasn't until I got to the door of the church with my matron of honor, a Scottish friend, and saw six little girls dressed in their communion dresses, carrying bowls of maize and bougainvillea, walk down the aisle in front of me. The choir chanted hymns in Chinyanja, and there were drums and it was all so beautiful that I felt my knees almost start to buckle."

Hope loved her work for the *Malawi Times*. Aside from attending press conferences with the other foreign correspondents – a stringer for the Associated Press and a reporter for the *Manchester Guardian* – called by the president, Dr. Kamuzu Banda, she covered social events, the opening of Parliament, and court hearings, working with a crime reporter to write stories of the trials. "The atmosphere in the newsroom was collegial, warm, and funny," Hope remembers. "I was the only female and the guys I worked with were like brothers to me." Before they left Malawi, Hope also had a job in Zomba, then the country's capital, helping to systematize the Law Library in Malawi's new Ministry of Justice.

At the end of Alvin's Peace Corps tour, Hope and Alvin moved to Cambridge, Massachusetts, where Al earned a business degree at Harvard and Hope found a job working in the state's Medicare office. Hilary, their first daughter, was born while they were in Cambridge. But their international adventures were just beginning. Al was hired by First National City Bank (now Citibank) for a post in Cape Town, South Africa – the first of 12 years of international postings for the bank, and life changing adventures for Hope. Happy to return to Africa, they left for Cape Town when baby Hilary was six months old.

In the next 12 years, Hope and Alvin, with the girls, as they came along, lived in South Africa, Zaire, India, and Thailand. Just when they were ready to end their expatriate years and bring the girls home to the U.S., Alvin was asked to return to Africa for one more tour of duty for Citibank in Monrovia, Liberia.

"I inhaled diverse cultures like cigarettes," Hope says. "In each place I learned something new, saw something new, smelled something new, and tasted something new every single day." Part of Hope's job, as a corporate wife in support of Alvin's work in each of these cities, was to act as hostess for visiting business associates and their wives. She would welcome guests at dinner parties, take spouses out for the day, entertaining them with tours and taking them shopping. This was all a part of Hope and Alvin's partnership in service to Citibank.

Each African country offered its own challenges and adventures. In Cape Town and then Johannesburg, they lived in a police state, under the control of the Afrikaner National Party, which had instituted Apartheid in 1948. Afrikaners, descendants of the original white settlers of Cape Town who worked for the Dutch East India Company, "carried a legacy of resentment and bitterness," Hope explains, "which exists to this day." They had suffered at the hands of the British Army in the Boer War. Through trial and error, Hope learned to negotiate the rules of Apartheid, protecting non-white servants from exposure during "whites only" hours in the suburbs, suffering the rebuke of a bus driver when she sat in a seat designated for non-Whites on the bus. At the same time, she says, "We had friends, Afrikaner, British, German, with whom we drove to remote beaches on weekends for 'braaivleis,' the Afrikaner version of barbecue, with lamb chops, sausage, and chutneys." These were distractions from the "deeper, darker issues we lived with, but we still debated those issues deep into the night with our South African friends." Some white neighbors were activists who stood on street corners, at risk to themselves, wearing black sashes to mourn "the death of constitutional law in South Africa," Hope notes. Heather was born in Johannesburg, four weeks before they moved on to their next post.

In 1970, Citibank asked Alvin to open a bank in Kinshasa, the capitol of Zaire and a boom town of Belgians, who had returned to the Congo to mine its natural resources under what had become a stable independent democratic government. Hope remembers Belgian bakeries and grocers, and sidewalk bistros, where they could enjoy a meal, Hope says, "on a shady street in Kinshasa on a sultry evening." The young woman who took care of the girls taught Hope how to dress in Congolese style, using nine meters of fabric divided into three sections – one for a long skirt, one to make a fancy blouse, and one for an elaborate head wrap.

The Hageman family left Kinshasa in 1972, and spent the next seven years in India and Thailand. In India, with a staff of servants in each household, Hope continued to host visiting business associates and friends. As the girls came of age, she enrolled them in British schools there and, with time on her hands, used her writing and interviewing experience to engage in volunteer projects. While in Bombay, she and another Citibank spouse created an English Guide to Bombay, sold in hotel bookstores for tourists, with proceeds to support the charitable activities of the American Women's Club. In Kolkata, she joined American, British and Argentine women in the Women's Friendly Society, a part of the East India Charitable Trust. "People were ready to pounce on expatriates for all kinds of organizations and causes," Hope says. This particular organization, an expansive network of services for a particular Indian population – the Anglo-Indian community – gave Hope all kinds of creative opportunities to support that community. Anglo-Indians, a mixed-race population dating from the days of the Raj, lived in "bustees," the squalid Kolkata slums. This population, which had been protected under British rule and given jobs on the railroads, were left behind, at the bottom of the educational ladder, after the British left India. Left on the streets and in poverty, the Anglo-Indians wore western clothes and spoke both Hindi and English.

Among other responsibilities Hope took on for the Women's Friendly Society – planning a fundraising gala, writing the program, helping design children's clothing for sale in the organization's fundraising shop – she became a caseworker, going into the bustees to interview Anglo-Indians there, in order to identify services they needed. "I had a driver who took me to the edge of the bustees, mazes of mud and garbage, and I would find my way to the people I was there to interview through the generosity of bustee residents eager to help me. I had not known such kindness in India before."

"What we could do for them was just a pittance," she added, "but it was something. We did what we could."

On their next bank assignment, in Bangkok, Hope took a docent course at the National Museum of Thailand, then joined museum volunteers in taking visitors on weekly tours. At the end of her course, Hope wrote a paper on some of the museum's holdings that captured the attention of a director, who asked her to contribute to a series of lectures for visitors.

"I think my Vassar education helped me project my thinking from the facts I was learning to the questions I had learned to ask," Hope says, thinking back. "I was able to expand my understanding, as Mr. Rumble had taught me."

Baby Shanti, Hope and Alvin's third daughter, was born in Bangkok. It was at about this time that "we realized that we wanted our children to experience life in the U.S., and that our ex-pat days were numbered," Hope recalls, "but we couldn't resist one last African posting, this time in Liberia." Liberia had been founded and funded by the American Colonization Society, "an odd alliance," Hope notes, "of southern slave owners and northern abolitionists" returning formerly enslaved Americans to Africa in 1820. In Liberia, Citibank serves as the de facto central bank of the country, and the culture of the country itself is startlingly American. They were in residence during the extraordinary Rice Riots in 1979 when, for the first time in 150 years, indigenous people protested the rise in the price of rice instituted by the elite descendants of former American enslaved people, who were in control of the government. "The Liberian Army proved more trigger happy than the rioters," Hope reports. "I crawled around the house through the night making sure my three girls were sleeping well away from the windows."

Monrovia was their last African posting, though they have traveled there often since. Hope says, "Though we have been back in the United States for more than 40 years, hardly a day goes by when I'm not reminded of our time in Africa. Al and I still use the occasional word in Chinyanja that conveys an idea more meaningfully in that language."

In 1980, they moved back to the U.S., to Deerfield, Illinois, their next assignment for Citibank. That move occasioned Hope's first-ever experience of culture shock. Deerfield, an affluent upwardly mobile suburb of Chicago, one that Hope says aspired to be the swankier Lake Forest, was an insular community by comparison to their seven homes that preceded it. When they bought a house in a cul-de-sac, the realtor introduced them to the neighborhood by leaving a card in neighboring mailboxes with the note that the Hagemans were relocating from Monrovia, Liberia. This caused alarm until the neighbors learned that Hope, Alvin and the girls were not themselves African. There was also a midwestern bias Hope and Alvin learned to negotiate: one new friend worried that Hope's girls might consider going "back East" for college. "What if she marries an Easterner!" Hope routinely prayed, "Please don't let me die in Deerfield."

They were there for eight years, and their reintroduction to American culture as a family meant that they had very full, very busy lives in Deerfield. Hope, who describes herself as a "klutz," says she watched her active girls running around the back yard, and thought, "I want those girls to have an experience I didn't have – I want them to be exposed to sports." So she turned to Alvin, a superlative athlete, who had turned down a draft by the Kansas City Chiefs after graduating from Williams, and said, "You need to get out there and play games with those girls, get them interested in sports."

It worked. The girls became involved in competitive sports in Deerfield, particularly swimming, and the community around those sporting events became like a second family, Hope says. She also points out that after years abroad with more household help than she knew what to do with, she now had to learn to run a household all by herself, shopping, picking up and delivering children, running errands. "I was very spoiled in Africa and Asia," she admits.

Still, Hope sought a community with which she had common ground in Deerfield. She found that community when she joined the League of Women Voters and its international relations group, six women with whom she could share her international experience, and whom she came to cherish. The

League, she explains, conducts issues research, tries to reach political consensus, and conducts voter registration drives. Through research, programs, and panels, and even a lobbying arm, the League works to have an educated electorate. "I wonder if it is not an anachronism now," Hope says. "There are so many organizations trying to do the same thing." Alvin likes to tease Hope by referring to the League as a "coven."

When the Hagemans left Deerfield to move to Westport, Connecticut, following another job assignment for Alvin, the Deerfield League's international relations group, as a parting gift, gave Hope a membership in the Westport League, and that gave her a good head start in their new, and now permanent, home. Asked if Westport was also a culture shock, Hope said, "No! I thought I'd died and gone to heaven! I was coming home to a place where everyone was well traveled and I didn't have to explain my life to anyone. I felt at home right away."

When they moved to Westport, the two older girls were getting ready to go to college, Hilary to Vassar, and Shanti was still a little girl in the Westport school system. Heather, the middle daughter, had by this time distinguished herself as a nationally competitive swimmer and would soon earn a swimming scholarship to Louisiana State University. Meanwhile, Hope jumped into League work, holding every office, serving on the Connecticut board of the League of Women Voters, organizing a symposium on international relations that she chaired for a few years.

Hope had no interest in looking for paid work at this point in her life. "I didn't feel a need to earn money on my own, or a lack of personal definition," she says. "I have to admit that while the women's movement was in full force, while I was in Africa and Asia, I had a very jaundiced view of feminism. I saw photos of women burning their bras, and I thought they were just opening themselves to mockery and satire." On the other hand, she tells a story of a niece watching the Miss America Pageant in the kitchen. Hope, without thinking too much, reached up and turned off the TV, telling the girl that watching that stuff would spoil her mind. So I guess there's something of feminism in me ..."

Hope and Alvin have been in Westport for more than 30 years now, and in that time, Hope served for eight years on the town planning and zoning commission, arbitrating issues around development and land preservation in a town with property values greater than those on Rodeo Drive in Los Angeles. But the effort she values most of all the projects she has been involved with has been the improvement and preservation of Sherwood Island State Park in Westport. Because of its beautiful town beaches on Long Island Sound, just five minutes from the center, the town's population doubles in the summer. Hope and a friend launched the Friends of Sherwood Island State Park in order to plan and raise funds for a Nature Center and other facilities that would make the park a welcome place for children and adults to enjoy Long Island Sound in the summer. "We now draw inner city families from three states to the park in the warm months. We hire high school and college students to provide guided tours of the natural habitat, and we work with the Friends of Connecticut State Parks to lobby the legislature for funding for the state's parks," Hope says. "It's the most gratifying work I have done." Through the League, the Friends of Sherwood Island State Park, and the planning and zoning commission, Hope now communicates on a first-name basis with Connecticut's state legislators.

Now, after years of hard work in all of these volunteer roles, Hope will devote her energy exclusively to Sherwood Island, an effort she views with the most pride, looking back. "I have to pass on my experience to the next generation," Hope says. "It's time to groom people to take over." She notes that it makes her laugh to think that her work, for which she has not been paid, easily takes 40 hours or more per week. Alvin hopes that Hope will start writing about her experiences. "I'd love to," Hope says. "I just need to find the time."

CHAPTER 10

Charting New Territory

"If it hadn't been for Ms. Asprey bringing computers to Vassar...well, it changed my whole life. We were able to flourish in a field that was just taking off..."

Elizabeth Ratigan

The social revolutions we toppled into during our college years were only part of our story. There was also the digital revolution, which some of us have spent a lifetime trying to grasp, even as it has profoundly altered our everyday lives. We were on the cusp of that, too.

During the four years that members of the Class of '65 were on campus, we typed our papers on manual typewriters. When we called home, we called on the hall phones installed, one to a floor, on each floor of the dormitories. We hand wrote letters to our friends. The first computer, the ENIAC (Electronic Numerical Integrator and Computer), had been built in 1943, the year most of us were born, at the University of Pennsylvania. But computers, as aids to computation or communication, were not part of our experience or our vocabulary. So when six math majors in the Class of '65, including Elizabeth Ratigan, took Math 385, "Studies in Digital Computing," and Math 289, "Independent Work in Computer Theory" during our junior year, 1963–64, they were taking the first computer courses to be offered at the college, and among the first computer courses offered in a liberal arts college in the United States.

The course was introduced to the curriculum by math professor Winifred "Tim" Asprey, a Vassar alumna, class of 1938, a woman much loved by faculty and students, who returned to teach at the college after earning a doctorate in math at the University of Iowa. Her fascination with computers – and friendship with, and encouragement from, computer pioneer Grace Hopper – had led her to take a sabbatical year from teaching to learn more about them, working at IBM's research laboratory, just down the road from Poughkeepsie in Armonk, New York.

The six classmates who took that first computer course at the IBM facility – and indeed the majority of the 26 math majors in the Class of '65 – about eight percent of the class – spent at least some time in their lives working as systems engineers or computer programmers, several as IBM employees – in jobs that didn't exist before we graduated from college. Some taught math, some worked in tech fields before and after raising children, or worked from home, thanks to the remote access provided by the Internet. Classmate Karen Doyle Walton had a notable academic career in mathematics education, in which digital expertise would be foundational. Having been admitted to Vassar after her junior year in high school in Johnstown, Pennsylvania, Karen was younger than most of her classmates. The math department, in the person of Ms. Asprey, provided a safe harbor for her, and she flourished there. After Vassar, Karen earned master's degrees in math and a doctoral degree in higher education administration while teaching mathematics and publishing articles on computer science. With her husband, Joe Walton, she raised two sons while working full-time. Karen was for 25 years provost and vice president for academic affairs at DeSales University in Pennsylvania.

Vassar had emphasized teaching math and science to women since its beginning, in 1861, when Matthew Vassar was encouraged by his sister to create a four-year college for women in Poughkeepsie. The first building on campus, the Observatory, was designed to the specifications of Vassar's first professor, astronomer Maria Mitchell. Mitchell, who taught at the college until 1888, helped the school enroll more math and astronomy students than Harvard during the latter half of the nineteenth century.

In an article about Asprey in the *New York State Mathematics Teachers Journal,* Karen Walton points out that there is a direct line of influence from Maria Mitchell in the nineteenth century to our Ms. Asprey in our era. Ms. Asprey's grandmother, class of 1882, "was encouraged to study science and mathematics" by Mitchell, and the grandmother in turn passed on her enthusiasm to her daughter, Asprey's mother, class of 1905, who also studied math and science at Vassar and passed the torch to *her* daughter ... which brings us to Winifred Asprey and, by extension, her students. Karen reports that during our tenure at Vassar, Ms. Asprey encouraged the college to purchase the computer that would be installed on campus, making Vassar the first women's college to own an IBM System/360.

Computer scientist Grace Murray Hopper, a math major in the class of 1928, who would become involved in creating the computer programming language COBOL (common business oriented language), came back to Vassar to teach in the math department after earning her Ph.D. in mathematics at Yale. She was a young professor at Vassar during Ms. Asprey's years as an undergraduate math major, from 1934 to 1938, and they became good friends. It was Hopper who gave Asprey an introduction to computers, inviting her to visit the computer laboratory where she did her work to show her "what they are and what they do," Asprey later reported. Inspired, she asked Hopper, "What do you think about Vassar getting into computers?" to which Hopper responded, "I've been waiting for you to wake up!" Which brings us to Elizabeth Ratigan, who credits those first computer courses, offered by the mathematics department during our junior year, with altering the trajectory of her life.

Computer Analyst: Elizabeth's Story

Elizabeth is a person who loves puzzles – jigsaw puzzles, sudoku and KenKen, crossword puzzles, card games that involve strategy, like bridge. While watching TV, she knits baby blankets with involved patterns that she then donates to hospitals and charities, now that her grandchildren are growing up. Tall, with a stately bearing and the complexion of a redhead, though her hair is now gray, Elizabeth leads a neat and orderly life, until very recently in a contemporary house, surrounded by bright colors. Like many residents of Washington, DC, she is focused on politics, starting every day with an exhaustive review of the news in the print press and on her preferred online news outlets.

Coming to college with a strong academic record from a prominent girls' school in St. Paul, Minnesota, Elizabeth assumed she would graduate and then get married. "I didn't know anything else. That's what my mother and her friends did." She found herself taking a lot of math courses but she did not feel like an outstanding student at Vassar. College grading was as humbling an experience for her as it was for other classmates, and Elizabeth at one point thought of leaving Vassar to become a secretary or work at Bonwit Teller's Department Store. Her father would not hear of it, saying emphatically, "I expected you to go to college and I expect you to finish." And math was beginning to get really interesting.

Ms. Asprey had arranged for Math 385 to be taught by a researcher at IBM. Elizabeth and her classmates went over to the IBM lab, a room fully occupied by a machine with a typewriter at the right. The computer was, for the time that they were there, for the exclusive use of the class. "I can't quite remember," Elizabeth notes, "but I think we input our programs on punch cards – there was a keypunch in the room to make changes to our programs when they didn't work." The room was isolated from the hubbub of cubicles and offices where the IBM professionals made daily digital discoveries. Elizabeth and the other students worked on the computers at the IBM offices, learning the fundamentals of their engineering, about adders and half adders and what happens when you input 1 and 0. From the first, Elizabeth loved the work, just as she loved mathematics. "I loved the logic involved in working on computers," she says, "working out the steps to make something happen, figuring out where it went wrong. It was like doing a puzzle."

In the spring of 1964, our junior year, Elizabeth was in another battle of wills with her father. Looking into the future, Mr. Ratigan, uncomfortable with this mysterious new field of knowledge, thought his daughter should become a teacher, an appropriate profession for women, which would always provide her a skill and employment. He urged her to earn teacher's certification after graduation the following year.

Elizabeth resisted. She was interested in continuing her programming work. A tug-of-war ensued. Fortunately, her father's old friend John Driscoll, head of the St. Paul Fire and Marine Insurance Company, took her side in the argument and offered her a summer job as a data processor. That summer, Elizabeth ran a sorter, operated like a telephone switchboard with wires and plugs, to sort information by column, or alphabetically, or numerically, for example. It was her first inkling that she might be a part of a whole new professional field. "The work in this entry-level job could be tedious," Elizabeth says, "but I loved the *processes* the machines used to sort the information." Mr. Driscoll took an interest in Elizabeth's progress, and she began reading about theoretical math and computers on her own. She began to feel a calling. "The summer job convinced me, after studying at IBM, that I wanted to do programming," Elizabeth says. In retrospect, though he had other ideas for her, she credits her father's influence and high expectations of her for helping her launch a career.

There were no new computer courses for her to take senior year, but company recruiters began to call at Vassar in the winter, setting up interviews for starting jobs. Elizabeth interviewed with the CIA (which was looking for smart secretaries), Bell Labs, and representatives of an organization called the Institute for Defense Analyses (IDA), who were particularly interested in the work Elizabeth had done at Vassar. She went to Washington, DC during spring vacation to visit the IDA office and she was offered a job there, starting at $6,300 a year, a good starting salary then. "I went for a job and found a career," Elizabeth says. It was unplanned, unanticipated, and very exciting.

IDA, located in Washington, DC, is a think tank established by a consortium of universities to serve the military. It researches problems defined by the Chairman of the Joint

Chiefs of Staff and the Secretary of Defense. To better understand the military's technological needs, faculty were sent through the institute and back to the academic world to help design new technologies to meet military requirements. Governed by a board of university presidents, IDA was created with the support of academic institutions to form a bridge between the Academy and the military. That never really happened. In 1968, the relationship between IDA and Columbia University was at the center of the student riots at Columbia, where students believed that the university had taken an immoral posture in supplying research for war materiel for the war in Vietnam. Disaffiliation from IDA was a principal demand of the student demonstrators. At Princeton University, students took control of the IDA building on campus, holding it hostage in another Vietnam War related demonstration.

The Institute has always worked across the military establishment and other government programs. Elizabeth, for example, wrote programs to run tests on metal detectors at airports, as hijackings became a crisis. Later, working with the computer language FORTRAN and computer modeling, she did strategic analyses directed at the Russian military, programs to target their nuclear weapons and other issues at the center of American foreign and military policy. It was exciting, and a year at IDA grew into 19 years. Much of the work was, of course, top secret. Elizabeth remembers, for example, when a colleague was assigned to track on an oversized plotter the path of the Viet Cong. Everyone on the IDA staff had to leave the computer room in order to assure the security of the program he was creating.

Public outcry about the Vietnam War grew with the American bombing of North Vietnam in 1967. The bombing further fueled an anti-war movement that had begun on college campuses just as we were graduating, and our generation took to the streets across the country. Elizabeth joined in that surge of protest, demonstrating almost every weekend, she says. If she felt a disconnect between her military work and her political views, that was okay with her. "Like other people in our office, I felt it was better for me to be doing the work than some war-loving lunatic." She noted that a number of the men in the computer group at IDA separated themselves from the Vietnam War in their own way, in that they had been able to avoid the draft for the Vietnam War, instituted by President Nixon in 1969, by getting a deferment while working there. Universities and their faculty were also beginning to rethink their support of the defense industry through IDA.

As her career developed at IDA, Elizabeth became more interested in systems programming, working *inside* the computer operating systems, learning and programming using machine language, designing improvements to the operating system. "It was tedious, detailed work, but I liked it," she says. "I can spot a typo a mile away," she adds, "and programming, to put it simply, is all about typos – getting the language right."

"In fact, that's why I feel that computer programming is, or was, a good field for women. The hallmarks of a good programmer are patience, persistence, attention to detail, pattern recognition, and logic, all qualities that women have at their command." Now, in the twenty-first century, though, "computer programming is a terrible field for women," she adds ruefully. Women in the computer industry are routinely dismissed, attacked online and made to feel unwelcome. "My theory," she says, "is that today's computing has grown out of gaming, an industry where guys often sit by themselves in dark rooms playing violent computer games. It's an inhospitable environment for women and today they have no clue that, in the beginning, this was an ideal field for them."

Writer Clive Thompson, whose article "The Secret History of Women in Coding" was published in the February 17, 2019

New York Times Magazine, concurs with Elizabeth's view that by the 1980s, women were pushed out of the field as the industry developed a distinctly male "geeky" profile for programming jobs, and became resistant and even hostile to hiring women. And in the culture, involvement with computers began to be defined by gender. Boys were more likely to be given personal computers by their parents. Fathers were more involved and mothers less engaged with computers, and girls got cultural cues that they were less able to do programming. The "cultural schism," Thompson notes, was reinforced in school and college computer courses.

"Women were among the field's earliest, towering innovators," Thompson says in his article. There was, for example, the first known "coder," Lady Ada Lovelace, the British mathematician who, in 1833, wrote perhaps the first computer program to help inventor Charles Babbage in his struggle to design a machine that would store information in its memory and execute "demands." Thompson highlights women who were "foundational in the prehistory of computing." These include the women of Britain's Bletchley Circle who operated the machines that helped decode the infamous German Enigma machine during World War II. And, of course, he mentions Vassar alumna Grace Hopper.

Thompson notes that women were assumed to have the kind of precise, "picky" mentality that was suited to coding. Men viewed writing code as a secondary, less interesting task. "The ENIAC women were among the first coders to discover that software never works right the first time – and that a programmer's main work, really, is to find and fix the bugs," Thompson writes. These "fixes" were at the heart of software development. Without the dedication of women and their willingness to do this work, computers may never have developed as they did.

Elizabeth confesses that earlier in her career, she was

neither interested in, nor spurred by, the women's movement. "I felt like I had a real job that was considered important, and I was treated as a professional." She had no trouble getting a job, her director encouraged her in her work and, so far, she had encountered no discrimination in the workplace. There was an equal mix of men and women in the computer group at IDA, though not in the Institute as a whole, and the field was new for men, too, so men and women were on a par competing for programming jobs in the beginning. She explains that there were two work groups at IDA – the computer group and the cost group. While the computer group was designing programs, the cost group was providing cost analysis to all the directors.

Soon, Elizabeth became the head systems analyst in the computer group at IDA, the person others would go to when they couldn't figure out what was wrong with their programming. When the head of the computer group, whom she served as deputy, left his job, it was not at all a sure thing that she would be named to replace him. She was surprised when she was. "It was a shock to have a female in management in 1979," she says. "At that point at IDA, there were four divisions, two groups, two vice presidents and the president. As head of a group, I was the only woman in management, and younger than most of the other leaders."

It was at this point in her career that she became aware of what could be called a kind of institutional sexism at work, and awakened to the structural aspects of the workplace that disadvantaged women. It was subtle, and it came less from the men in the office and more from the support staff. The security guards, the secretaries and others in a support role treated the men with great deference and respect, calling them Mr. So and So, while they approached Elizabeth with a friendly informality, complaining to her about other directors, calling her Liz. Her experience points to the strengths of women in the workplace – making co-workers comfortable – that is at the same time a weakness, in that they are less respected. "Nobody saw their informality with me as improper or disrespectful," Elizabeth says. "But it was at this point that I decided to drop my nickname and ask to be called Elizabeth, an attempt to create at least a little formality around my position." Like many of us, Elizabeth also found herself sidelined in management meetings, ignored or discouraged from contributing her opinion. "All my male colleagues had Ph.Ds. I didn't have the credential they had for bringing in business to IDA."

It was when, as director, she had to fight to get adequate pay for the computer operators that she began to see parallels between their salary gaps and her own compared to other directors. "I went to my boss to ask for better compensation for myself, and when he turned me down, I would just say 'Oh, okay,'" she says. She was fighting for her group but had not learned how to fight for what she thought *she* was worth. "The way we were raised had a huge impact on how we dealt with men in the workplace. If Dad said do something, you did it. If Mom said do something, you thought about it."

By the time she was in her mid-thirties, it occurred to Elizabeth that, contrary to her earlier assumptions, she might not marry. She wasn't particularly troubled, though, like others of our class might have been. Her life was full, she felt that the work she was doing was important and she felt fulfilled doing it. She didn't have a lot of time for a social life. "I worked a lot of late nights," she remembers, and her Aunt Ruthie, to whom she was very close, provided a compelling model of a vibrant life as an unmarried woman. Thus, it was not surprising to Elizabeth that if there were going to be any romance in her life, it would happen at work. And she had great friends at the office.

One of those office friends was, for example, Phil Gould, a

brilliant colleague and intellectual sparring partner whose research she had been programming for years, occasionally scrapping over how the work should be done. Phil, a polymath with many interests, had gone through a difficult divorce. In Elizabeth he found a good sounding board, willing to tease him about his attempts to modify his appearance now that he was single again. "Oh, for God's sake, Phil, take off those contact lenses and put your glasses back on," she would say upon seeing him squint and blink with his attempt at a new, more attractive look. Eventually their relationship became a romance. They married in 1980 when Elizabeth was 37, and had a rich life in which they shared Phil's children with his former wife – a life that ended only when Phil died, too early, from cancer 30 years later.

In 1984, Elizabeth was ready to move on from computers. She had been going to George Washington University part-time, where she earned a master's degree in operations research, studying methods to improve decision making and efficiency in the workplace, and she was looking for a new challenge. It was at about this time that she got a call from someone named Steve who was interested in her experience – with computers, as it happens. They arranged to meet "at an anonymous building near Tyson's Corner," Elizabeth says, across the Potomac River from Washington in a thrumming suburban Virginia business development. There he took her into a computer room, where they talked about computers – IBM, Control Data, Univac, Digital Equipment – and he was pleased to learn that Elizabeth was particularly familiar with the computers Russians used for weather ... and nuclear programs.

Steve said he had an interesting job to offer Elizabeth, with a small, specialized group working on special projects. He was inviting her to join the Central Intelligence Agency (CIA). And she did. Over 15 years, Elizabeth had intriguing jobs, she says, working with different CIA groups to develop a next generation of computing equipment for the Agency, moving on from Wang computers to other systems, and developing programs whose purpose was to attempt to retrieve data from foreign computers.

There were a lot of women employed at the Agency, but again, not in computing. Elizabeth's new job enabled her to continue to use her now considerable computer expertise. But there were new challenges. Like many employers in the country, the CIA wanted to address problems of race and gender in the advancement of women and people of color. Elizabeth and her colleagues went through diversity training, and the Agency began to include participation of women and minorities on promotion panels. It was at this point, with the kind of training that the Agency had offered, that Elizabeth began to see more clearly the fairness issues that the women's movement had been addressing for the last 15 years, and became more interested in standing up to correct those issues. "The diversity training had a big impact on me," she remembers. "I had been so passive about asking for equal pay for my own work, and now I realized the huge impact those same equal pay issues had on minority employees."

Phil, too, helped Elizabeth to be more confident about her abilities and worth. When the CIA offered her an assignment running the signals intelligence operations at the Agency, she at first said "No, I can't do it." She would be working with radio operators, an essentially male working group, and she didn't feel that she would have authority with the group. Phil said, "Do you think any man would say that?" No, she thought, and she took the assignment.

Elizabeth retired from the CIA at 63, going on to serve on boards and volunteer to read for the blind, work at the DC Historical Society and travel with Phil until he died. What she took away from her work, in addition to the satisfaction of having gotten in on a new field as it was being born, was a sense of mastery. "My work was wonderful for my ego," she says, summing up her professional life. "I knew I was good at it, and I was able to help a lot of young professionals along the way."

CHAPTER 11

Making Sense of It All

*"I used to give some seminars on juggling a career and mar-
riage ... my conclusion was that there was a cosmic balance.
Perhaps by the end of your life, it would have cosmically
balanced out ... I mean for a while there, the women's movement talked very seriously about balancing things like it was
somehow a scale and every morning you would see if it was,
you know, and then you would fine tune it. I think it's impossible and I think it's a crock ..."*

From The Bank Street conversations

The sons and daughters of members of the Class of '65 are
still trying to find balance in their work and personal
lives. But fortunately, of the many accidental pioneers in our
age cohort, two classmates – Debbie Michaelson Kolb and
Mary Ann Mason – have dedicated much of their professional
lives to work/family challenges. Mary Ann, who in 2000 was
named the first woman graduate dean of the University of
California at Berkeley, devoted much of her research and

writing to issues of work and family balance, in service to the generation after ours – the pioneer generation, as Mary Ann called us. Her book *Mothers on the Fast Track,* co-written with her daughter Eve Mason Ekman, offers an analysis of the obstacles to professional young women seeking balance between work and family as they pursue "fast track" careers. Using statistics available in 2007, when *Mothers* was published, Mary Ann reported, for example, that despite increased enrollment among women in graduate and professional programs – law school, medical school, business school, Ph.D. programs – 17 percent of partners in law firms were women, 15 percent of executive leaders in communications were women, and of CEOs in Fortune 500 companies, only seven percent were women. Statistics for women in medicine and academic careers offer a similar picture, due to the fact that many women choose to remain in midlevel professional careers in order to balance family demands with work.

Mary Ann's own story inspired her to address the difficulties facing this new generation of women in the workplace. After college, and encouraged by a mentor, Vassar history professor Carl Degler, she earned a Ph.D. in history, thinking that she would teach. Instead, married and a new mother, Mary Ann moved with her husband to Berkeley, California, where he had secured a teaching job, but the prospects for a teaching position looked grim for her. She decided to get a law degree, which would offer more geographic flexibility, in the event that the family moved again. But in her first year as an associate at a law firm, she found she was "unable to deal with the demands of work and home," Mary Ann reported in her book. "I could not manage the long hours required to succeed as an associate." She divorced, left the law and, feeling a sense of failure, spent a decade teaching part-time at Berkeley and writing books on issues of women and the law, and women and work. She was on a "mommy track," in that she was working, but in a role that would not advance her career. During that time, Mary Ann had remarried and had a second child. Her book *The Equality Trap,* written in that period, caught the attention of her Berkeley colleagues and, in her 40s, she was offered an entry-level position as a history professor at Berkeley. She was lucky, she says, to get a second chance in an era that was "opening the door to women without changing the demands of the workplace ... setting mothers up for failure." It was one that led her back to the "fast track" as graduate dean.

As a professor and as graduate dean, Mary Ann was able to witness the growth in the number of women getting academic degrees. Her research on women and work led her to meet and serve as a guide to many young women trying to balance careers with family obligations, and who want to stay on the fast track. *Mothers on the Fast Track* suggests solutions to employers to help working mothers, for example, during the "make or break years" at the beginning of demanding careers. These solutions include family-friendly policies, making it possible for mothers to come back to the workplace without penalty after a break for childcare. Her book encourages working mothers to keep working – if they can – so that they stay on track; and to protect "mother time" by saying no to meetings and travel that take them away from home, and by negotiating flexible work time, including work from home.

Debbie Kolb has spent her career helping to make sense of the world of work for women. As a professor at the Simmons College School of Management, Debbie centered her research on mediation and negotiation in the workplace. She began to focus on work/family issues when she was asked by colleagues to participate in a Ford Foundation-sponsored research on company policies that related to work and family balance. Together with a team of researchers, Debbie and colleagues

Lotte Bailyn and Joyce Fletcher interviewed employees at three different companies, asking what their principal work issues were. Of the men and women, both young and older, an overwhelming majority identified issues related to work and family. Working with the companies, Debbie and colleagues identified time- and morale-eating barriers to getting work done during the workday that left employees working into the night or taking home work on weekends. Though the company may have instituted flexible time policies, employees were afraid to make use of them because the company culture encouraged competition among employees that rewarded dedication exhibited in long hours. In the study, they asked the question, "What is it about how work is done that makes it difficult to integrate work and personal lives."

Their study at Xerox Corporation, for example, revealed "second generation gender bias," as Debbie calls it, referring to an initial attempt – one that wasn't working – to accommodate working parents. In reality, the company's work structure rewarded 24/7 dedication to the job and viewed employees who were not able to put in long hours as less dedicated to Xerox and less suitable for leadership positions. Though the company offered flex time to employees, no one asked for it, for fear that such a request would have a negative impact on their careers. Debbie and Bailyn and the team looked for hidden barriers to efficient work that would allow employees to go home to their families at the end of the workday. Engineers, for example, spent a great deal of time in meetings, leaving them little "quiet" time to get their work done on their own. That translated into longer hours to complete the interrupted work. The team helped Xerox to change how it worked so that employees could find balance between work and family. In another company, a product development team was failing to come up with creative new ideas until, with the help of Debbie and colleagues, the company modified time-eating meetings, schedules, status reports, and management reviews, and restructured the workday so that there were quiet times and interactive times. The quiet times yielded more creative work and members of the team were able to go home to their families at the end of the workday.

These initiatives represent the beginning of a new way of thinking to accommodate the needs of families with two working parents, as is the norm now. Debbie and Mary Ann have been midwives to cultural change in the workplace.

The Academic: Debbie's Story

Debbie Michaelson Kolb, diminutive and intense, is an unexpected feminist, as she actively resisted the "feminist" moniker until later in her career. She was one of several classmates who, with no "ring by spring" and no immediate plans to marry, went to Boston with friends after college, got an apartment and enrolled in the Radcliffe secretarial course. That course led to a first job – as a secretary – in the economics department at Harvard, along with a number of women who, she says wryly, "were similarly under-employed." That led to other jobs, more degrees and more jobs over time until, to sum up Debbie Kolb's career with a kind of shorthand, one could just list her titles: Deloitte Ellen Gabriel Professor for Women in Leadership (Emerita) at Simmons College in Boston, MA; Founder of Ford Foundation funded Center for Gender in Organizations at Simmons College School of Management; Former Executive Director, current Co-Director of Negotiations in the Workplace Project at the Program on Negotiation at Harvard Law School. There have been other titles, too – Faculty Research Fellow at Stanford University's Clayman Institute for Gender Research, in 2008–2009, faculty at INSEAD, European Institute of Business Administration in

Fontainebleau, France, and visiting professor at MIT's Sloan School of Management. Debbie is the author or co-author of seven books on negotiation in the workplace, three of them focusing on strategies for women at work.

This was not the career – or life – that Debbie expected or even wanted when she was a student at Vassar. Her father, an obstetrician, and her mother, a graduate of nursing school, had no particular expectations of Debbie as a professional, nor did Debbie herself while she was an undergraduate at Vassar. Though she had started her life as a nurse, Mrs. Michaelson was a stay-at-home mom for her three daughters. But, Debbie notes, "She was a very active volunteer, eventually running Planned Parenthood in their county of Long Island. It seemed like a natural fit for my mother, with three daughters and having been a nurse," Debbie adds.

"I was my father's favorite child," Debbie remembers, "and I have always thought of him as the most supportive (but also combative) of my parents." They were proud of Debbie, and wanted her to be happy. She notes that her mother came to help Debbie when her children were born, but in sum, they were not that close. With some self-examination, however, Debbie has come to see her mother's influence as a woman, particularly regarding her work with Planned Parenthood. This was a pattern I would notice among the women I interviewed – a strong father who exerted a dominant influence on his daughter, and a mother who, perhaps suffering from a feminine mystique, receded into the background, appreciated for her strength in retrospect.

A small woman, full of kinetic energy, from Rockville Centre, New York, on the south shore of Long Island, Debbie admits she worked only as hard as she needed to earn a bachelor's degree in history at Vassar. Without that engagement ring in June 1965, Debbie moved to Boston and her first job as a secretary at Harvard.

Through connections from her first job, Debbie moved on
to work at Abt Associates, a Cambridge consulting firm that
hired men with Ph.Ds. to write consulting proposals for
clients, and women with degrees from Seven Sisters colleges
like Vassar to do the work executing the contracts. It was
interesting work. Abt often had government contracts, consulting for the Office of Equal Opportunity, the Department of
Labor, and other government agencies, and Debbie worked as
a technical assistant, evaluating programs. It was at Abt
Associates, inspired by co-worker Regina Herzlinger, that
Debbie began to think seriously about pursuing a master's
degree in business administration. Herzlinger, who was the
first woman doctoral student at Harvard Business School and
her first mentor, encouraged Debbie to think about graduate
school for herself. Debbie took a graduate management
admission test (GMAT) to see if this was a realistic plan, and
she surprised herself by doing very well. But with the uncertainty that afflicted all of us after four years earning lower
grades than we had anticipated at Vassar, she felt that her
college record might not impress admissions people in a
university MBA program. Besides, "I had never taken a
calculus course at Vassar," Debbie says, acknowledging that
familiarity with calculus would help her get into business
school, "so I took courses in both calculus and accounting, and
was astonished to discover that I loved the subject matter."

During her first summer in Boston, Debbie became friends
with Jonathan Kolb, whom she had met through a classmate
from Vassar. By the end of the year, she and Jonathan, who
was in his first year at Harvard Medical School, were a couple.
Like so many of our generation, Debbie and Jonathan were
politically active – they joined anti-war marches in Boston,
protesting the war in Vietnam, an effort she notes that
eventually "brought down a president!" (Lyndon Johnson,
wearied of the war and the controversies surrounding it,

surprised the country by announcing that he would not run for re-election in 1968.)

But Debbie was not particularly engaged in the women's movement. Her interest in getting an MBA degree, which would prepare her for what was still a man's world, was borne out of a genuine academic interest in studying business. She would resist the political call to feminism for much of her career, until she ultimately found herself by default a spokesperson for women in the workplace, and used her own professional expertise to train women for leadership.

Debbie and Jonathan married in 1967, and in 1970 moved to Denver, Colorado, where Jonathan took a three-year residency in psychiatry. They were anxious to spend this time away from the east coast, in a new environment. It was in Denver that Debbie began her graduate work, earning an MBA at the University of Colorado. Because she had, by this time, a four-month-old baby, her son Sam, she pursued her degree by taking night courses at the university campus in Denver. After what she terms her "mediocre" grades at Vassar, she was delighted to get an A on her first paper, and she began to believe she would do well in graduate school. At home, she found support among women by joining other mothers in playgroups and she did her "consciousness raising" while drinking coffee in the morning and wine with the mothers in the afternoon.

In her final year in the MBA program, Debbie took courses at the Boulder campus, including some doctoral seminars. These latter courses sparked her interest in pursuing a Ph.D. By the time they returned to Boston, Debbie had an MBA degree and plans to pursue a doctorate in organizational management, and Jonathan was ready to take a job in psychiatry at McLean Hospital. She was pregnant with their second child, Elizabeth, and Sam was ready for nursery school. They moved to Boston's South End, where they found a wonderful neighborhood of young professionals. It functioned like a village, a community where young families supported each other, children all played together, "and any time you needed something, you could ask a neighbor for help," Debbie says. It gave Debbie the support she needed to keep going with her graduate education, even as she awaited her second child.

She applied to Ph.D. programs at both Harvard and MIT's Sloan School of Management, and was accepted at both. Her focus would be in organizational sociology, a study of how organizations shape the experiences of people who work there. Debbie's work at Abt Associates had piqued her interest in social sciences, and she was interested in studying people in organizations, looking at workers in context, not in studying behavior through psychological experiments in a laboratory.

Debbie chose MIT because they were willing to allow her to pursue her Ph.D. at her own pace, enabling her to balance her family responsibilities with her studies. Even though Harvard could see, at her meeting with its doctoral committee, that Debbie was very pregnant, Harvard would not allow her to be a part-time student. It was a general graduate school policy at Harvard, having nothing in particular to do with women in the program. They were concerned that part-time candidates would spend their time earning money as consultants instead of focusing on their studies.

In informing Harvard that she would choose the program at MIT, Debbie told the committee, "You are making a mistake in not allowing your Ph.D. candidates more flexibility," and she laughs recounting that she got a call from Harvard while she was in the hospital, having just delivered Elizabeth, that they would accept her as a part-time candidate after all. But she had made up her mind. As it turned out, Debbie was the only woman in her class at MIT. All of this could have led to an awakening interest in feminist issues, but "I was not there yet," Debbie says.

One thing led to another in shaping Debbie's career. A friend in the South End, Arnold Zack, who was a renowned labor arbitrator, invited Debbie to accompany him to a labor negotiation in which he was involved in Belmont, a Boston suburb, between the teacher's union and the school committee. What she thought might only be a modestly interesting evening ultimately became the subject of her Ph.D. dissertation, which won the Zannetos Prize at MIT for outstanding doctoral scholarship, and her first book, *The Mediators,* published in 1983. Debbie found mediation and the whole process of conflict resolution between warring sides of a work issue to be fascinating. Through the 1980s, Debbie researched and wrote about mediation and negotiation in the workplace. At the time, there was an explosion of interest in negotiation and mediation, and her book gave her a prominent place in the field.

On the advice of another mentor, Lotte Bailyn, professor of management at MIT's Sloan School, who urged her to take her time writing her dissertation, Debbie spent seven years completing her work, at the same time managing the lives of her two children. While she was working on her dissertation, she began teaching at Simmons College, a women's college in Boston, in an executive program for women who were middle managers. Again, surprisingly, her interest in working at Simmons had nothing to do with an interest in women's issues in particular, but it put her in the right place at the right time. In fact, because she had earned attention in her field as a result of her award-winning book and her appearances as a speaker on mediation at professional conferences, she was recruited for several faculty jobs at prestigious business schools, so Simmons wasn't her only choice. But the other jobs would have involved leaving Boston, and by this time Debbie and Jonathan were embedded in their community and moving was not a realistic option. She decided to remain at Simmons, an all-women's business school.

In 1987, while she was teaching at Simmons, Debbie was asked to be the associate director of the Program on Negotiation at Harvard Law School, in addition to her teaching at Simmons. There, as the only woman in the program, Debbie became the "instant expert on gender," the person who was asked to come talk about the differences between men and women as negotiators in other professors' classrooms. "It was a subject I had not really considered before," Debbie says.

At the same time, like other women in our class, she was by this time experiencing her own gender issues in the workplace. Evaluations from her seminars were generous with positive comments, but if students didn't like what Debbie proposed, they would go directly to the male director of the program, triangulating communications so that he would then come to her with the students' complaints. It dawned on Debbie that "this gender stuff might be an opportunity for me ... I began to read feminist literature," she says, "and that's when I got interested in the subject."

But the real turning point came when Debbie was invited by Lotte Bailyn to participate in work/family research projects funded by the Ford Foundation on company policies that related to work and family balance. Though work and personal life did not have a direct relationship with Debbie's research, which was mediation and negotiation in the workplace, it offered her a new way of thinking about gender. Bailyn had become a treasured colleague, one that Debbie still meets regularly for breakfast "and professional nourishment," she says. Bailyn was particularly interested in issues raised by conflict between work and family responsibilities and she has written widely about it.

A critical member of the team of researchers Debbie and Bailyn assembled was Joyce Fletcher, whose work really changed Debbie's understanding of gender. Joyce studied the work of women engineers for her dissertation. She identified ways in which women in the workplace took on work that was invisible – building collaborative teams and other hidden "relationship" work that went unrecognized and unrewarded. Her work, *Disappearing Acts,* shows how the women who were in leadership roles never got credit for it. It was "disappeared" and hence the women were not considered for leadership roles.

From the beginning of her studies in organizational sociology, Debbie has used ethnography – that is, she has collected stories of people in the workplace, and their experience in negotiating for what they need or want from their work. Because she taught in an all-women's program, she collected many stories of the trials and successes of women negotiators. In a way, that seems a particularly feminine way of doing research – through relationships – and it is one that has translated into seven very readable and relatable books on negotiation, and many hundreds of talks at companies and conferences around the world.

Debbie was always learning from the women and men she met at conferences, and from the subjects of the stories she collected. The more she learned about the unintended consequences of workplace policies for women, the more she honed her work to address those issues. She came to see that women needed to be better advocates for themselves in negotiating for position in the workplace, but also to establish connection and collaboration – to demonstrate that what was beneficial for them was also beneficial for the organization. She was able to point out that negotiation between companies and employees that led to better integration of work with personal lives would be helpful to *both* men and women, and to the long-term stability of the organization. Her research also showed that women, however, have to deal with a kind of organizational backlash that men do not experience. Behavior that is seen as "strong" in men is "shrill," or "pushy," in women. While men are encouraged to act for their own benefit, exercising their ambition without guile, women are expected to show concern for others, and pay a social cost in organizations if they don't. It is difficult to deal with this double bind. One strategy Debbie suggests is to name that it is happening. She points to an article by Sheryl Sandberg in which she describes a woman negotiating a salary: she starts by saying that the other person might see her as pushy. That strategy of "naming" the issue helps to disarm the listener. Another approach is to provide the reasons you are doing something that is in the organization's interests – "I am pushing hard for my group." Debbie notes that women constitute the majority of college graduates, and make up 50 percent of middle management, but are still relatively rare in senior corporate positions.

As Deloitte Ellen Gabriel Chair of Women in Leadership at Simmons School of Management, Debbie held an honor named for an accountant at Deloitte who instituted a leadership development program that moved women into partnership positions there. In 1994, Simmons received a grant to create the Center for Gender in Organizations (CGO) at the School of Management. With this grant, CGO became a center for innovative work on gender in organizations. Key scholars in the field like Joyce Fletcher, Lotte Bailyn, Robin Ely and Debra Meyerson were fellows in the program. According to Debbie, it was an amazing run. Under the auspices of CGO and the School of Management, this team created leadership development programs for women that drew on the research of CGO. Deloitte, Time Warner, Morgan Stanley and others sent their high potential senior women to these programs.

As Simmons started to have financial problems, Debbie took a buy-out in 2011. She has built on the work she did at

Simmons and now runs leadership programs (in collaboration with her CGO colleagues) for leading companies, and she teaches about gender and negotiations around the world. In addition, she's passing the baton to her daughter Elizabeth, who earned an MBA in 2001, and has been working in startup firms in Portland, Oregon, while raising two of Debbie's grandchildren, Isaac and Eli. Debbie's son Sam, father of Debbie and Jonathan's other two grandchildren, Jacob and Alexandra, has been a high-tech engineer at Survey Monkey, in California.

The good news is that "there are role models now for the next generation," Debbie points out, noting that she and Jonathan offered a model for their children. Now, their son is an active, engaged parent involved in childcare, as Jonathan was, and their daughter is following in her mother's footsteps. It's both flattering and rewarding to know that we have provided role models for our children, one of the benefits of struggling through all those years of juggling work and family, and a reward that our mothers largely didn't have.

Elizabeth, like her mother, has spent time teaching and lecturing at conferences about women in the workplace. "I want to work with you," Elizabeth told her mother, and together they presented at a workshop on negotiation for women in technology in Portland, Oregon.

Her most recent book, *Negotiating at Work*, published in 2015, combined Debbie's two specialty areas – gender and negotiation. The book considers the second generation gender issues that create challenges for women, and provides negotiating strategies and tactics to deal with them. What Debbie believes (and hopes) is that when people negotiate about second generation issues – not being considered for a promotion, not getting credit for invisible work – these will be small wins that subtly change organization practices.

The work goes on.

CHAPTER 12

Where Are We Now?

"A customer looked at a vase I had made, a tall vase with a tapered neck. Admiring it, she asked, 'How long did it take you to make that vase?' Thinking about it, I said, 'Forty years.'"

Susan Jacobs '65

C lassmate Susan Jacobs has been making pottery in a studio on Capitol Hill in Washington, DC, for most of her life since college. With the mastery and experience she has acquired, she now spends much of her time teaching pottery techniques to people like her who want to use their hands, wet clay, and a pottery wheel to make something beautiful. Debbie Kolb echoes Susan's observation in describing the process of writing her most recent book, *Negotiating at Work*, published in 2015. "It was a few years in the writing," Debbie says, "but many more years in the evolution of its ideas."

Mastery and experience – and wisdom, we hope – are the gifts of age. How are we using those gifts now? And are we making up this phase of our lives, too? Perhaps unique to our generation of women is the fact that we are the first to have struggled with the fear of a loss of identity when we left our careers behind. Women, traditionally, knew their identity – they were caregivers throughout their lives. It is the men who have struggled to define themselves outside of work. Before our 50th Vassar class reunion, classmate Karen Doyle Walton conducted a reunion survey of 875 alumnae in the Classes of 1965 at Vassar, Mt. Holyoke, and Radcliffe colleges. Among the very interesting nuggets of data Karen uncovered in survey responses from more than 400 alums was a collection of thousands of narrative comments the women made in response to some questions. To retirement questions, respondents reported fearing a loss of identity once they stopped working. They also worried about missing colleagues and losing the structure work gave to each week. They worried that they would be bored.

When I stopped working at 63, I had all those fears. I signed up for classes, volunteered for too many causes and joined too many boards, just to be sure my time would be filled with meaningful activity. I soon discovered that I had overbooked my time, and began to peel myself away from some of those commitments. I began to enjoy the more flexible structure of retirement, and I found a rekindled curiosity about art and history and literature that I had not been able to indulge since college. And I had a plan to write a book about the family letters I had found in an old box in my parents' house. I wrote that book and settled into a newly defined structure to my life.

I can say that we are all still active and learning. Debbie Kolb, for example, is working with her daughter to create training films produced and directed by LinkedIn, which offers online business courses. Debbie is willing to help her daughter create leadership videos, and they have made one, but she believes she should not be the professor on camera anymore.

"I know I am a good teacher," Debbie says, "but I'm too old!" She will help write the course, but notes that a gray-haired older teacher is not what young professionals want to see. "It's time for a new generation, and Elizabeth will do very well."

Dorsett Edmunds is still earning a living as an acupuncturist, with clients calling to fill her calendar. She also teaches zero balancing techniques, a kind of energy-based therapy, and goes to conferences to speak to practitioners about zero balancing and paths to well-being. When she is not doing that, or taking care of herself with a rooftop yoga class just in time for the Arizona sunset, she is volunteering to leave food for migrants at the Mexican border, or working with the refugee community in Tucson. Lately, Dorsett has also taken out her hammer dulcimer, built for her by her then soon-to-be husband in her North Carolina days, when mountain dulcimer music captured her fancy. Dorsett says she is rusty, but with practice she will accompany Christmas carols at church this year.

In addition to her continued involvement in the New Canaan Domestic Violence Partnership, Dede Bartlett has used her corporate career to remain a leader and mentor for young women. As a Woodrow Wilson Visiting Fellow, she has been invited to spend a week on college campuses, along with astronauts, authors, judges and other Fellows with corporate experience, talking to undergraduates about life beyond college. After her years mentoring Vassar students, she now has the immense satisfaction of working with Vassar, the architects, planners, and staff, to bring her support of the next generations into a tangible reality in the new career center on the Vassar campus, named for her.

To satisfy her curiosity about her own family's piece of American history, she worked with genealogical researchers to write a three-volume history – *Discovering My Lost Family: The Unexpected Journey of an American Woman*. As an extra, she has written a book, *The Things They Loved,* reporting what she learned about 12 inherited objects – silver, furniture, a baby dress, a Bible, rugs – that have come down through the generations, and the stories they tell about her family.

Now, after years of hard work in many volunteer roles, Hope Hageman will devote her energy exclusively to Friends of Sherwood Island State Park, an effort she views with the most pride, looking back. With the Nature Center at the park now operating, and a cadre of summer volunteers trained to teach children about their natural environment, and the growing threats to it, she feels an urgency to assure its continuation. "I have to pass on my experience to the next generation," Hope says. "It's time to groom people to take over."

Sylvia Drew Ivie continues her health advocacy work as Special Assistant for Community Affairs, working for the president of Drew University. The coronavirus pandemic put her at the center of the crisis response, focusing on getting Black and Latinx people in the community tested for the virus. "We tried to test about 1,000 people a day. We had the only walk-up clinic in the area. We allowed them to register on the same day and we talked them through the process," she reports. "When patients tested positive for the virus, we called to tell them, and we put them in touch with outpatient care. Thirty percent of our patients have no health care." Looking back at her life, Sylvia says, "I never had a master plan. I have been surprised at the opportunities that have been given me." She has derived energy in doing work with a mission to serve justice, and she is grateful for the chances she has had to pursue that mission.

Ros Anderson Nesticò, still an assessor for the baby friendly hospital program in Italy, has become interested in feminine spirituality. Raised in the Episcopal church in Tallahassee, she has spent most of her adult life attending a

Catholic church in Florence with her husband Aldo. Her interest was piqued when she read Sue Monk Kidd's *Dance of the Dissident Daughter*, an exploration of a transition in Kidd's spiritual life in which her religious (Christian) experience collided with nascent feminism. The book traces Kidd's own awakening to how women submerge themselves in caretaker roles for men and families, then "wake up," perhaps in midlife, to a desire to listen to their own needs. Ros found a women's spiritual group in Turin, engaged in shamanic or traditional spiritual practices using dance circles, and drumming to achieve enlightenment through meditation. She has learned to drum and now has three drums that she treasures – one, a Lakota Sioux drum, one a drum she made herself with horse hide, and one given to her by a close friend. "I am drawn to it," Ros says.

Elizabeth Ratigan now uses her considerable digital skills to do historical research on behalf of her family and as a volunteer for the Washington Historical Society. She serves on community boards, as does Moira Burke, who has only just given up practicing ophthalmology to pursue cultural interests – opera, ballet, theatre – in Tampa and other Florida Gulf cities.

It was in an accident of timing that my classmates and I graduated from Vassar in 1965 just as American culture was turning somersaults around us: we were a cohort of women delivered into a world reinventing itself. War and American imperialism, civil rights, the environment, sex, and women's place at home and in the workplace were all on the table. Looking at this small sample of women in the Class of '65 at Vassar, what are the common threads from which we might draw conclusions? How did we create lives that juggled the competitive pressures we faced? First, we were all lucky. All nine of us had the support of our families, a good education and enough financial resources to make that education happen. Seven of us have graduate or professional degrees in addition to a college education. All of us, I think, took advantage of our good fortune to push ourselves into a world undergoing stunning change.

Of the nine women whose stories are told here, all of us married, and all had children or stepchildren, meeting those early expectations for a domestic life. Six of us have had one sustaining long marriage, whether or not we had careers. Three of us divorced, with two second marriages. Two of us were widowed too early. With the exception of Sylvia Drew Ivie and Moira Burke, we all believed that we would work for a few years, just until we fulfilled our destiny to be well-informed wives and mothers, and could then stay at home. All of us were surprised by our lives. All of us, at one point or another, were making it up as we went along.

Of course, we had help along the way. Interestingly, most of us had strong fathers (in my case, a brother), who helped set our expectations of life, who provided obstacles we had to overcome, who taught us how to overcome them, either by resisting us or encouraging us, sometimes both.

In the absence of, and in the shadow of her famous father, Sylvia Ivie's mother did all of that and more. Dede Bartlett's mother gave Dede some important guidance as she began her adult life. For most of us, our mothers had a less dominant, less directional voice in our lives. Perhaps they were victims of the feminine mystique Betty Friedan ascribes to the 1950s, trapped in a domestic role that did not allow them to presume much more than to keep us safe and clothed and fed.

Some of us were fortunate to have mentors in the workplace, both male and female. Debbie Kolb was lucky to have been in a community of professional women who worked together to break new ground in their field. The men who helped us were generous. We learned from men, but we have, as women, been able to be mentors to women in the generation that has followed us.

Going back to the Women's March on January 21, 2017, where I began this book, classmates reporting in from the marches that day in Philadelphia, New York, Hartford, Washington, DC, Boston, Los Angeles, Boise, Idaho, London and Oxford, England, most often used joy and hope to describe their experience in this latest gesture of participation in the political life of the U.S. What brought joy was the sense of community that participants felt in those marches – a sense that we have come a long way, bringing men with us, and children and grandchildren. One classmate mentioned that her favorite sign that day said, "I can't believe we're still fighting for this shit!" But we are, and that's good news, too. To borrow from Shakespeare's *Henry V*, it was like our St. Crispin's Day in reverse – an opportunity to look back at what has been accomplished. The world we see in our late seventies is in many ways profoundly different from the world we entered in our twenties. And we took part in making a difference.

There has not been enough change: our sons and daughters have had to struggle to balance work and family, as we did; racism is still too painfully present in our lives; war is always on the horizon; damage to the environment has only gotten worse. All of those are existential challenges that we, with our age and education and experience, want to be a part of meeting. Sure handed as we feel now, we are not ready to stop using our hard earned power and voice to be agents of change. We old ladies are signing petitions, calling our representatives, going to town meetings, engaged in political and community activity. Are we more active, more engaged than our mothers were, because of the era in which we came of age? I think so. Do we feel "younger" than the generation of women who came before us? Well, yes, but also, I think, having had a lifetime filled with rich opportunities along with daunting challenges, we also are more willing to embrace our age.

It may be comforting to the next generations to know that there are aspects to aging, as women, that are very satisfying. If I may presume to speak for women of my age, I would say that now that we are older, we are less intimidated. The loss of physical strength and the onset of diseases of the aging are inconvenient and sometimes overwhelming, but if our minds are still acute, life is good, and we feel a new kind of strength and power and invulnerability. And the world is still very, very interesting.

Perhaps at this age we have less to lose, which gives us a clarity of purpose we didn't have in our twenties. Have we made our last trip to the barricades? Not likely.

Once more unto the breach...

ACKNOWLEDGMENTS

There are so many people who helped me write *Making it Up* – women, like me, in their eighth decade, who had to reach back in their memories to help bring alive an era of social revolution for women that, like it or not, changed everything for everyone. My thanks go first to Jane Carney Scully, who shared with me the transcripts of the Bank Street conversations, stored away since she reported on them in the reunion book for our 25th class reunion in 1990. Her generosity allowed me to revisit those conversations and use them to help give form to a book idea that I had been carrying around in my head for all those years.

I want to thank the women of the Vassar Class of '65 who shared their memories with me, beginning with the eight women who trusted me with a candid, thoughtful retelling of their life stories: Dede Thompson Bartlett; Moira Burke, Dorsett Edmunds; Hope Oliker Hageman; Sylvia Drew Ivie; Deborah Michaelson Kolb; Rosalind Anderson Nesticò, and Elizabeth Ratigan. I hope that I have represented our conversations well, and honored their trust in me in reporting on them. I am also grateful to other classmates who volunteered pieces of their stories, fortifying a kind of ethnography of the era that I wanted to bring to life: Deborah Detchon Dodds; Mollie Ramsey Foster; Susan Jacobs; Barbara Baylis Luehring; Ruth Levy Perles; Lynn Povich; Karen Doyle Walton; Mary Mapes Watson; Mary Williams, and, posthumously, through their own books, Susan Gordon Lydon and Mary Ann Mason.

I hate to think of the rich stories of classmates that I have not told here. Some day it might be interesting to conduct an expanded examination of the stories I missed through some kind of dialogue or sharing mechanism like a blog, but the technical expertise it might require may be beyond me.

I want to acknowledge the trove of information collected in the Vassar Encyclopedia, under the direction of Vassar's College Historian, Dean Emeritus of the College and Professor Emeritus of English Colton Johnson. I invite everyone to go on the website at Vassar.edu, and explore it.

Thanks go to my writing companions Kathleen Frank, Roger Friedman, Barbara Kazdan, Sarah Lesher, Susan Tobias, and most especially Sara Mansfield Taber for tapping here, chipping there, and patiently helping buff the material until it had the shape and direction I wanted. Thanks to Megan Turner, Alex Kale, and the delightful team at Atmosphere Press for all their help in turning this project into a book.

Most of all, I thank the people who keep me afloat, especially my husband, Henry Roemer McPhee, and my daughters Katrina Holmberg and Erika Holmberg, women I admire so much for doing it all so beautifully as wives, mothers, professional women, and bright spirits. Helan Går!

BIBLIOGRAPHY

To put our stories in the context of our times and circumstances, I found the following books, some written by classmates in the Vassar Class of '65, to be very helpful:

Cobble, Dorothy Sue, Gordon, Linda, and Henry, Astrid, *Feminism Unfinished,* Liveright Publishing, 2014

Collins, Gail, *When Everything Changed*, Little Brown & Co., 2009

Coontz, Stephanie, *A Strange Stirring*, Basic Books, 2011

Cott, Nancy F., *The Grounding of Modern Feminism*, Yale University Press, 1987

Friedan, Betty, *The Feminine Mystique*, W.W. Norton, 1963

Gillette, Howard, Jr., *Class Divide: Yale '64 and the Conflicted Legacy of the Sixties*, Cornell University Press, 2015

Horn, Miriam, *Rebels in White Gloves: Coming of Age with Hillary's Class – Wellesley '69,* Anchor Books, 1999

Jaffe, Rona, *The Best of Everything*, Penguin Books, 1958

Kaledin, Eugenia, *Mothers and More: American Women in the 1950s*, Twayne Publishers, 1984

Kolb, Deborah ('65) and Porter, Jessica, *Negotiating at Work: Turn Small Wins into Big Gains*, Jossey-Bass, a Wiley brand, 2015

Kolb, Deborah ('65), and Williams, Judith, *The Shadow Negotiation: How Women can Master the Hidden Agendas that Determine Bargaining Success,* Simon and Schuster, 2000

Lemons, J. Stanley, *The Woman Citizen: Social Feminism in the 1920s,* University of Virginia Press, 1990

Lydon, Susan Gordon ('65), *Take the Long Way Home,* Harper San Francisco, 1994

Mason, Mary Ann ('65), *The Equality Trap*, Transaction Publishers, 2002 (original copyright 1988)

Mason, Mary Ann ('65), and Ekman, Eve Mason, *Mothers on the Fast Track*, Oxford University Press, 2007

McCarthy, Mary ('33), *The Group*, Harcourt Press, 1989

Pells, Richard, *War Babies,* Cultural History Press, 2014

Povich, Lynn ('65), *The Good Girls Revolt,* Public Affairs Books, 2012

Sanford, Nevitt, ed., *The American College: A Psychological and Social Interpretation of the Higher Learning,* John Wiley & Sons, 1962

Stearns, Peter N., *Battleground of Desire*, New York University Press, 1999

The Vassar Encyclopedia, an "online work in progress" under the direction of Vassar's College Historian, Dean Emeritus of the College and Professor Emeritus of English Colton Johnson.
https://www.vassar.edu/vcencyclopedia/

ABOUT ATMOSPHERE PRESS

Atmosphere Press is an independent, full-service publisher for excellent books in all genres and for all audiences. Learn more about what we do at atmospherepress.com.

We encourage you to check out some of Atmosphere's latest releases, which are available at Amazon.com and via order from your local bookstore:

The Great Unfixables, by Neil Taylor

Soused at the Manor House, by Brian Crawford

Portal or Hole: Meditations on Art, Religion, Race And The Pandemic, by Pamela M. Connell

A Walk Through the Wilderness, by Dan Conger

The House at 104: Memoir of a Childhood, by Anne Hegnauer

A Short History of Newton Hall, Chester, by Chris Fozzard

Serial Love: When Happily Ever After... Isn't, by Kathy Kay

Sit-Ins, Drive-Ins and Uncle Sam, by Bill Slawter

Black Water and Tulips, by Sara Mansfield Taber

Ghosted: Dating & Other Paramoural Experiences, by Jana Eisenstein

Walking with Fay: My Mother's Uncharted Path into Dementia, by Carolyn Testa

FLAWED HOUSES of FOUR SEASONS, by James Morris

Word for New Weddings, by David Glusker and Thom Blackstone

It's Really All about Collaboration and Creativity! A Textbook and Self-Study Guide for the Instrumental Music Ensemble Conductor, by John F. Colson

A Life of Obstructions, by Rob Penfield

Troubled Skies Over Quaker Hill: A Search for the Truth, by Lessie Auletti

Down, Looking Up, by Connie Rubsamen

ABOUT THE AUTHOR

Selby McPhee was a staff writer and editor at schools, universities, and other educational institutions including Tufts University and the National Association of Independent Schools (NAIS), where she was marketing vice president. A freelance writer, McPhee has published articles in a variety of print and online publications.

McPhee's first book, *Love Crazy*, (Martin Sisters Publishing, 2013) was inspired by a box of letters marked "Personal letters of Mr. and Mrs. J. J. Fleming," with the admonition "to be destroyed unopened," in her parents' house.

McPhee lives with her husband in Potomac, Maryland.

Learn more at www.SelbyMcPhee.com.